Boot Up Rescue

Thanks to my old mum, Jane and the kids for putting up with my own bouts of ill temper when a PC plays up and Becky and Susannah at the Telegraph for their encouragement.

Boot Up Rescue

The Daily Telegraph
FIRST-AID GUIDE FOR YOUR COMPUTER

Rick Maybury

TEXERE
New York • London

Copyright © 2002 Rick Maybury

Published in 2002 by

TEXERE Publishing Limited
71–77 Leadenhall Street
London EC3A 3DE

Tel: +44 (0)20 7204 3644
Fax: +44 (0)20 7208 6701
www.etexere.co.uk

A subsidiary of

TEXERE LLC
55 East 52nd Street
New York, NY 10055

Tel: +1 (212) 317 5511
Fax: +1 (212) 317 5178
www.etexere.com

Project managed by Macfarlane Production Services, Markyate,
Hertfordshire, England (e-mail: macfarl@aol.com)

A CIP catalogue record for this book is available from the British Library

ISBN 1-58799-126-8

Printed and bound in Great Britain by TJ International Limited, Padstow,
Cornwall

Contents

Introduction

The next time your PC throws a wobbly or keels over – and it will – I hope *Boot Up Rescue* will encourage you to have a go at diagnosing and possibly fixing the problem. At the very least it should reassure you that it almost certainly be revived, you are not alone and that there is plenty of free expert help available.

The really disturbing thing about the modern Windows PC is that the more you know about what goes on inside the box, the more improbable it seems that they work at all . . .

The collection of bits and bobs that go to make up a PC – the electronic hardware – is fantastically complicated but surprisingly reliable. It's the software – the operating systems, programs and applications – and accessories – printers, scanners, modems, etc. – that cause most of the trouble. The point is PCs have become victims of their own success. The 'open architecture' design that has made the PC so affordable and accessible also allows just about anyone to build them, write programs and make peripherals.

The permutations of software and hardware – of varying degrees of flakiness – that can be used on a PC are virtually limitless. Then there's the human factor. When was the last time you sat down and actually read the instructions, before installing a new piece of software or hardware? It's hardly surprising that occasionally something goes wrong.

The trick is not to panic, and to know when to stop! Most PC problems start out simple and fixable but rapidly descend into chaos as users resort to increasingly desperate measures. I know it's tempting but I can say, with absolute certainty, backed up by many years of personal experience, that frantically tapping keys and clicking the mouse almost never effects a cure.

It would be impossible to catalogue every PC fault, a thousand new ones are invented every day, but they do tend to fall into a relatively small number of categories and the flow chart in Figure 1 should help you to find your way to a solution or a source of help reasonably quickly.

Finally, a word or two of warning. This book is only concerned with PCs using the Microsoft Windows operating system, specifically Windows 95,

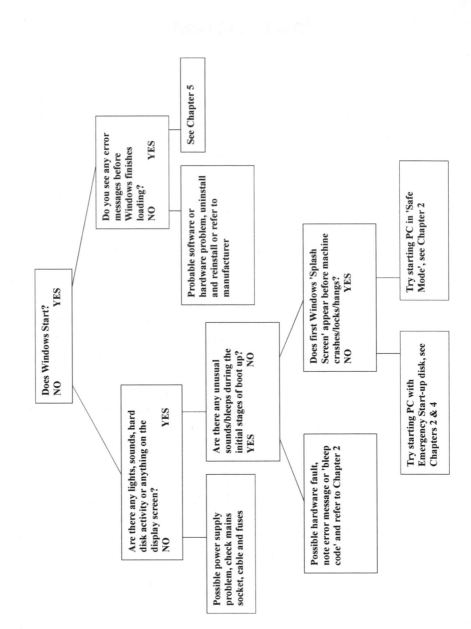

Figure 1

98 and ME, with occasional references to Windows NT and 2000. *Boot Up Rescue* can't help with your software problems, other than the core applications found on most PCs, and it goes without saying that if you've got a faulty Mac or handheld/palmtop PC you are unlikely to find any answers here.

CHAPTER 1

Switching on

For most of us switching on a Windows PC is only marginally more exciting than watching paint dry. The machine bleeps, lights wink, the hard disk chatters, lines of apparently meaningless text and pictures of clouds come and go, then, all being well, a minute or so later the desktop appears.

GETTING STARTED

Problems during boot up are very common and cause a great deal of frustration. Often the solution is reasonably straightforward, but knowing where to find it can be difficult and, in desperation, a lot of users end up making matters even worse, so it's worth knowing a bit about what is supposed to happen when you press the 'on' button on your PC.

Immediately after switch-on a small program called the BIOS (Basic Input Output System), which is stored in a 'non-volatile' memory microchip on the computer's main circuit board or 'motherboard', carries out a series of diagnostic checks called Power On Self-Test or POST. These make sure that the main electronic components, memory chips, keyboard and disk drives are all connected and working properly. By the way, having the BIOS program stored in a memory chip – as opposed to being held on a disk drive – means that the checks can be carried out, even if there are problems with the disk drives or other components.

If you watch the screen during these early stages usually the first thing you see is information about the PC's video components followed by details concerning the BIOS program; then there's a name check for the PC's central processor unit or CPU. If everything is okay you will hear a single beep from the PC's loudspeaker and the first part of the boot up sequence continues with the memory test. You'll see some numbers whizzing around on the screen, stopping at something approximating the size of your PC's random access memory (RAM) capacity. In other words

```
◐Award Modular BIOS v4.51PG, An Energy Star Ally
  Copyright (C) 1984-99, Award Software, Inc.

#401A0-0106a

PENTIUMIII-MMX CPU at 633MHz
Memory Test :   65536K OK

Award Plug and Play BIOS Extension v1.0A
Copyright (C) 1995, Award Software, Inc.




Press DEL to enter SETUP
01/09/01-i440LX-P2L97A-00
```

EPA POLLUTION PREVENTER

Power On Self-Test (POST) memory check; this PC has 64Mb of memory

if your PC has 64 megabytes of RAM the memory test number should read '65536K OK'. If you're wondering how it arrives at that particular value, that's because a kilobyte or a thousand 'bits' of information is actually 1024 bits, thus a megabyte would be 1,024,000 bits, times 64 equals 65,536,000 or 65536K.

During this part of the proceedings you should see a message on the screen to the effect that if you press the 'Del' key (sometimes F1 or a combination of keys), the PC will go into the 'setup' menu. This is a set of controls for the BIOS program and a no-go area for novices. It contains lots of critical settings that can very easily stop your PC working or make it misbehave in ways you wouldn't believe! If you're interested, we'll be taking a closer look at the BIOS program in Chapter 6.

The BIOS then goes on to identify the floppy and hard disk drives and any other drives attached to the PC and instructs the PC to load a set of start-up or 'System' files into its memory. The first place it looks for them is floppy disk drive A. You may have noticed that if you've inadvertently left a floppy disk in the drive from a previous session you will be prompted to 'press any key to continue' and boot up resumes as normal.

Checking floppy drive A: first is an important safety feature because it means you will still be able to boot up your PC, even if the system files on the hard disk drive are missing or corrupted. In order to do that you need an 'Emergency Start-up' disk. If the software on your PC was pre-installed an emergency start-up disk should have been provided with all the other disks and documentation, otherwise you are prompted to make one when you use your PC or Windows for the first time. If you haven't got one you should make one right now. Go to Add/Remove Programs in Control Panel, select the Start-up tab and follow the instructions. We'll look at how to use it in more detail in Chapter 2.

Having confirmed that there is not a start-up disk in drive A: the PC now looks for system files in a special area of the main hard disk drive called the boot sector. Incidentally, this is a common hiding place for viruses, where they can remain undisturbed and do the maximum amount of damage, so make sure you have a virus checker program on your PC, and that it is kept up to date.

System files – whether on a floppy disk or drive C – contain information about the PC's configuration and initiate the 'disk operating system' otherwise known as DOS (aka Microsoft DOS or MS-DOS, see Chapter 4). DOS tells the processor how to communicate with and process the files contained on the rest of drive C, organise its memory and look after all of the input and output devices attached to the PC. When DOS has finished loading, an instruction in the start-up files tells the PC to begin loading Windows.

Now the fun really begins. Windows is a huge program comprising thousands of files the first of which is a real monster called the Registry (another topic covered in Chapter 6). This is a massive database containing everything the PC needs to know about Windows, your PC's hardware and peripherals plus the programs stored on the disk drives and your preferences for the way Windows and all the other programs are set up. Suffice it to say a lot of problems can occur at this stage if the Registry is corrupted, but it is checked automatically and if there's a problem it can load one of a number of previously saved Registry files from the last time your PC booted up successfully. After the Registry has been installed Windows next loads a series of configuration files also stored in the boot sector (config.sys, autoexec.bat, etc.) which may also contain instructions for other programs, such as a virus scanner, to start loading. More configuration files follow, then comes the last major trouble spot, Windows drivers. These are scores, sometimes hundreds, of small data files requested by the Registry and configuration files that Windows needs to communicate with various bits of hardware, printers, the monitor, programs and so on. Finally, all being well, there's a welcoming 'ta-da' fanfare from the loudspeakers, the desktop appears and you're ready to start work...

WHEN THINGS GO WRONG

A PC that refuses to boot is one of life's more stressful experiences; when it happens to you – and it will – stay calm and take comfort from the fact that you are not alone; 99% of Windows PC users have, or will at some stage suffer the same fate. You may also be relieved to know that most start-up problems can be resolved fairly easily, but please note that physical violence and abusive language definitely does not help...

Something you don't want to see; if the Scandisk window appears there may be something wrong with your PC

As we have seen, a lot of things have to happen before the Windows desktop appears on the screen and although the boot up sequence is a complex business it can be broken down into two fairly distinct stages: part one is before the first Windows 'splash' screen appears. If an error message appears or the machine freezes before Windows begins loading then the fault is most likely to be concerned with the BIOS program or a fault with the hardware (motherboard, memory chips, disk drives, etc.). Thankfully hardware faults are quite rare and generally quite easy to resolve.

If something goes wrong after the first Windows screen then it is almost always due to Windows or a software problem. We'll round off this chapter with a brief look at some of the commonest hardware-related problems that occur immediately after switch on. In Chapter 2 we'll look at how to resolve problems that happen during the latter stages of the boot up process.

The obvious suspect in a totally dead PC (i.e. blank screen, no lights, stationary fan and no disk drive activity) is a loose mains cable, blown fuse or a problem with the power supply module. The fuses in the mains plug (and sometimes on the back of the PC) are easy to check, but if one has blown, make sure you replace it with the same type. If it blows again there's a more serious problem, probably concerned with the power supply. They can be repaired but usually it's quicker (and cheaper) to have it replaced. If you attempt it yourself (it's not a difficult job if you're handy with a screwdriver), make sure you get the correct type, both in terms of mechanical fit, motherboard type, and power rating.

Assuming power is getting through, the first sign of trouble happens a second or two after switch on; normally most (but not all) machines emit a single beep from the internal speaker to confirm that the first part of the POST test was carried out successfully. If you hear more than one beep, or a repeating pattern of beeps, that is a fault code which requires investigation. We'll be looking at that in more detail in Chapter 5.

One very common, and serious sounding boot up error message is 'CMOS Checksum Error' or 'Invalid Configuration', 'press F1 to continue'. After pressing the F1 key the machine will boot up normally, but you may well find that the clock in Windows is wrong, or losing time. This bizarrely worded message usually points to a dead or dying battery on the motherboard that is used to keep the PC's internal clock ticking when the machine is switched off or disconnected from the mains. Replacing the battery is not usually a difficult job, though on some machines it can be tricky to get to and is best left to an engineer.

One of the scariest error messages is 'Cannot read from hard disk C:' or something similar. In fact total hard disk failure is comparatively rare nowadays and the most likely cause is a loose cable from the motherboard to the disk drive. If you're familiar with the innards of your PC you may be able to fix the problem yourself. Switch the machine off at the mains socket (but leave the plug in so the case remains earthed) and remove the lid. Touch the metal case to dispel any static charges that may have built up on your body or clothes as these can damage the sensitive microchips inside your PC. Check the power and data cables going into the back of the disk drive and onto the motherboard.

A somewhat rarer condition, sometimes brought about by a long period of inactivity, is hard disk 'stiction' where the disk drive mechanism becomes stuck. If you cannot hear motor whine or chattering coming from the drive it is sometimes possible to get things moving again by lightly tapping the side of the hard drive case with the handle of a screwdriver. Nevertheless, take any kind of mechanical problems with your PC's disk drives – including strange noises – as a warning, and replace it before it fails completely.

Problems with the PC's random access memory (RAM) modules are quite common and they can be difficult to track down as they don't always show up during the POST check and can therefore look like a software fault. However, multiple bleeps from the PC during boot up are often a sign that there's something amiss, as are error messages that include the words 'Page Fault'. Fortunately they are fairly simple to resolve, if you are an experienced PC user and not averse to opening up your machine. If you suspect a memory fault and your PC has more than one memory module, try removing one at a time, or if you have access to a PC with a similar spec that uses the same kind of memory module, try substituting one or more of the modules.

If your PC makes it to the first Windows splash screen and then hangs, crashes or displays an error message, then the chances are the problem is software related, and we'll try to sort it out in Chapter 2.

Q&A **Real world problems**

Cool sounds?

Q My computer started grunting about once per second through the external speakers after booting up. This lasted for a few seconds, stopped and then started again several times. I restarted the computer but the sound persisted. It was not affected by the volume control for the speakers and the microphone was switched off. I shut everything down for a while and it was back to normal when I rebooted later in the day. What could be the cause and should I do something about it?
D.B. via e-mail

A The fact that the grunting noise occurs at boot up, isn't affected by the volume control and eventually goes away points to a dry bearing on the power supply or processor cooling fan, warning of imminent failure. You can easily confirm that by switching off or disconnecting the speakers and see if it still happens. If so, replacing the fan or power supply module isn't a difficult or expensive job but it's best left to an expert if you're not familiar with your PC's innards.

Black power

Q My computer has taken to showing me a black screen at every opportunity. Unless I am doing something the screen disappears after about 60 seconds, also when running Error check and Disc defrag. The process keeps stopping and starting again and takes forever to complete. Is there anything I can do to keep this black screen from appearing?
G.K. via e-mail

A The chances are you or someone else has been fiddling around with the power management settings on your computer and the monitor is going into power save mode. Go to Start > Settings > Control Panel and click on the Power Management icon. On the Power Schemes tab change the 'Turn Off Monitor' setting from 1 minute to a higher value, 30 minutes, say, or 'Never', depending on your pattern of use.

Trash the splash

Q I know that the Windows shutdown graphics can be found as logos.sys and logow.sys in the Windows 98 folder, but I'm stumped trying to find the file that contains the graphics of the Windows splash-screen that comes up when the PC is booted. I would be very grateful if you could point me to the file and make my PC my own, and not Bill Gates'. . .
A.M. Peterborough

A The opening Windows screen is called LO.sys but it may be hidden away inside a protected folder so you won't be able to get at it. However, you can easily replace it with an image of your choice using Windows Paint or your preferred paint program. Open the image, change the size to 320×400 pixels (don't worry about the odd shape) give it the name 'logo.sys' and save it in the root of the C: drive as a 256-colour bitmap. Windows will automatically use this instead of LO.sys, provided the attributes are correct. To revert to the original Windows splash screen simply delete, remove or rename your logo.sys image.

On message

Q I have had many a discussion about leaving my Windows 98 computer switched on virtually permanently when not in use. It goes into a standby mode, i.e. it goes to sleep. I have some worries when although it is presumably not working I hear a slight buzzing, which I presume is the fan working: why should this be since the CPU is not working? Alternatively it may be the sound of the transformer in the power pack. Whatever it is I feel some concern, perhaps I should switch off after use! Recently when it is in sleeping mode I have pressed any key to start – this does not wake it up. Eventually with some degree of apprehension I switch off at the mains and then turn it on again, only to get the message that it is checking the main disk for errors, as I did not switch off in the correct manner. This puzzles me; would you please offer some advice.
M.W. via e-mail

A Unless you have a good reason to keep your PC switched on all the time – to receive incoming faxes, etc., – then there is little or no point leaving it in standby mode, other than to save you the minute or two delay whilst the machine boots up. It's far better to switch it on in the morning or when you start work and only switch it off when you have finished for the day.

Although the CPU is idle in standby mode the power supply is still operating and on some older machines – without all of the latest power management facilities – the fans in the power supply and on the CPU chip continue to operate. In standby mode the PC still draws a few watts and components that are active will have their lives shortened. It is also a waste of power and apart from adding to your electricity bill, on a global scale millions of idle desktop PCs sitting around doing nothing is not helping the environment. Scandisk is set to run automatically when Windows 98 isn't shut down correctly. It's a safety feature, and you should let it get on with its work as it could help to repair files corrupted by the incorrect shutdown.

Regional conflict

Q   Every time I boot up my PC I get a message that states 'Are you still in the UK' to which I have to answer yes in order to proceed. Can you advise how I can get rid of this message?
Guy Davis, via e-mail

A   The PC is clearly confused, probably by conflicting language and keyboard settings. Check Regional Settings and Keyboard in Control Panel or put the thing out of its misery and answer yes. . .

CHAPTER 2 **Crash recovery**

*Faced with a dead PC that refuses to boot or load
Windows, there are two things you can try to get it
up and running – three if you count prayer ... –
however, the recommended strategy is to use your
emergency start-up disk, or try starting Windows in
Safe Mode. Also in this chapter we'll look at what
to do if Windows loads, but with error messages.*

EMERGENCY START UP

The all-important 'system' files stored in the 'boot sector' on the hard disk
are surprisingly vulnerable and can easily become corrupted by you, a virus
attack or belligerent software installed on your PC, but whatever the cause
your PC and Windows cannot function properly without them. The
emergency start-up disk contains a set of basic system files for your PC, so
if your PC hangs during boot up and there's an error message relating to
system files, switch off, pop your start-up disk into the drive and switch it
back on.

What happens next depends on what version of Windows you are using.
The Windows 95 Start-up disk is not especially helpful; a few moments after
loading the PC displays a black screen showing a few lines of apparently
meaningless gobbledegook and a flashing A: prompt. The machine is now
in DOS mode (see Chapter 4) from where you may be able to get Windows
going – if the files are undamaged – but at the very least you will be able to
run a series of checks using diagnostic and repair tools on the start-up disk,
and possibly recover files or documents.

Windows 98 and ME users get a lot more assistance from their disks. It
boots the PC and creates a temporary 'Ramdrive' in the PC's memory. This
is a kind of virtual hard disk drive, used to hold all of the tools and drivers on
the floppy disk. The Ramdrive becomes disk D: all other drives on the PC
are moved up a letter. (Don't worry, everything returns to normal once the

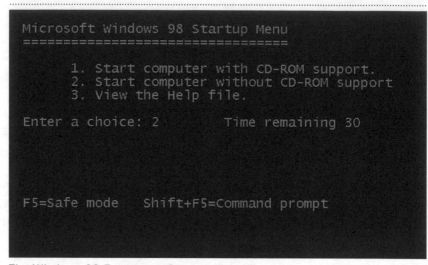

The Windows 98 Emergency Start-up disk gives you
three choices; in most cases option 1 is the one to
go for

PC boots up under its own steam.) The start-up disk gives a choice of
opening a detailed help file, starting Windows in Safe mode (more about
that later) and accessing help and resources on the Windows 98 installation
disk. The CD-ROM drive should be accessible since the start-up disk loads
the necessary drivers, but don't forget it will have been moved up a letter
(i.e. if it was drive D: it now becomes drive E:).

The 98/ME Start-up disk also includes a number of diagnostic and repair
utilities plus a 'Cab File' extraction tool that can copy compressed 'cabinet'
files from the Windows installation CD-ROM to your hard drive. There is
also a useful 'Readme' file, which is worth looking at, even if your PC is
behaving normally; you never know when you're going to need it!

If the system files are successfully loaded you will see an A: prompt on the
screen: before you do anything else it's a good idea to run two simple tests on
the hard disk drive and its filing system. The first is Scandisk, which looks
for defects on the disk drive and the files it contains and attempts to repair
simple faults. To start the program type 'scandisk' (without the quotation
marks) after the A: prompt and press the Enter key. It may take a few
minutes, and it's usually worth accepting any offer to carry out repairs. If
you're not in a hurry you can accept the offer to conduct a 'Full Surface
Scan' which will highlight any deep-seated faults on the hard disk drive,
though it could take an hour or more. The other test is Checkdisk (type

chkdsk at the A: prompt) and this carries out a quick health check on your hard disk's filing system. Again it will report errors and offer to fix them.

Once Scandisk and Checkdisk have passed your disk drive fit for duty you can try to start Windows. Type in 'win' (without the quotation marks of course) and press the Enter/Return key. If that doesn't work, change the drive letter by typing 'C:' then type 'cd Windows' (cd is a DOS command for 'change directory'). The screen should now show C:\Windows >, now type 'win' and press Enter and all being well it should load; if it fails to load or crashes, then it is time to move on to stage two, Windows Safe Mode.

SAFE MODE

In addition to reviving a dead PC, Windows 'Safe Mode' can also be used to solve a lot of the problems that generate error messages whilst Windows and other critical files are loading. Safe Mode bypasses the configuration files and start-up programs, which cause most problems and loads only the bare minimum of drivers for the monitor, keyboard and mouse. These should be enough to get Windows up and running, albeit with limited functionality.

To enter Windows Safe Mode press the F8 key (on some models you may have to press the Ctrl key) after the first round of POST/BIOS checks, before the 'Starting Windows' message appears on the screen. A moment or two later the boot up sequence stops and you will see a menu, with six

```
Microsoft Windows 98 Startup Menu
=================================

   1. Normal
   2. Logged (\BOOTLOG.TXT)
   3. Safe mode
   4. Safe mode with network support
   5. Step-by-step confirmation
   6. Command prompt only
   7. Safe mode command prompt only

Enter a choice:4




 F5=Safe mode  Shift+F5=Command prompt  Shift+F8=step by step confirmation
```

Safe Mode, one of the most useful troubleshooting
facilities in Windows

numbered options (seven in Windows 95 and four in Windows ME). We'll look briefly at each one in turn, and how they can be used to diagnose and solve problems.

Option 1 (all versions) is Normal mode; use this if you entered Safe Mode by mistake; select it by pressing 1 on the keyboard, press Enter and the normal Windows boot up sequence will resume.

Option 2 (all versions) is 'Logged (\BOOTLOG.TXT)'. Selecting this will also make Windows resume normal loading but at the same time it creates a text file (called bootlog.txt) which is stored in the root directory of the C: drive. This file records all of the actions during the loading sequence and notes whether or not each operation was successful; this detailed record, which you can save to a floppy disk, read using a Windows Notepad or a word processor, may help you or an engineer to pinpoint an obscure fault.

Option 3 (all versions) is Safe Mode, which loads Windows but with a basic configuration. The words 'Safe Mode' appear in each of the four corners of the desktop (which may be in black and white) and a warning message pops up. Click OK and loading continues. Resolution will be set to VGA standard (600 × 400) so the icons on the desktop and Start menu may look bigger than usual and some programs and peripherals might disappear from the desktop or stop working. Don't worry; when you have fixed the problem and Windows resumes normal operation, everything will be restored though you may have to manually reset things like the hidden taskbar and small icons on Start menu features on the Setting menu. Safe Mode in Windows 98 starts a 'Trouble-shooter' that provides immediate access to a very useful ME utility called System Restore that can return the machine to a previous 'known good' configuration. More about what you can do when the PC is in Safe Mode in a moment.

If the PC fails to start in Safe Mode it could be the work of a virus (see Chapter 9), though it is possible that there is a problem with the crucially important Registry system files. Windows 98 and ME have a Registry checking utility, which can be run from the DOS prompt after booting the machine by using the emergency start-up disk. At the A: prompt type 'scanreg'. Windows 98 and ME automatically make backup copies of the Registry every time Windows loads successfully. By default five copies are kept and these can be restored from MS-DOS mode by booting your PC using the Start-up disk. At the A: prompt type 'scanreg /restore', then choose a backup from which to restore your Registry.

Option 4 (option 5 in Windows 95) is potentially one of the most useful diagnostic options since it asks you to confirm each step of the loading sequence. Simply type 'Y' for yes at each step. If it freezes jot down the message and restart the machine in Safe Mode again. This time when you reach the suspect step type 'N'. If Windows then continues to load you will have a pretty good idea of where the problem lies. The message should point to a Windows driver or a recently installed application, which you can remove or re-install once Windows finishes loading, or from Safe Mode.

Safe Mode option 4 in Windows 95 is for PCs that are connected to a network. It is similar to option 3 but it loads extra files that will allow the PC to access the network, so you can carry on working if necessary.

Option 5 (Option 6 in Windows 95, not available in Windows ME) is Command Prompt Only. Try this if you can't get Windows to load in Safe mode. This starts the PC in MS-DOS mode (see Chapter 4).

Option 6 (option 7 in Windows 95, not available in Windows ME) is Safe Mode Command Prompt Only, which also starts the PC in DOS mode but leaves out Windows start-up files, so Windows cannot be loaded. Once

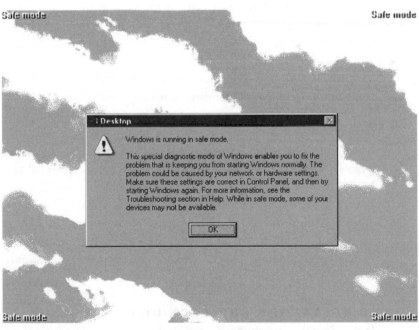

Windows Safe Mode; don't worry if the display looks
a bit odd

again this is not available in Windows ME; instead the option to start the PC in DOS mode is on the emergency start-up disk (press F5).

Whilst in Safe Mode (Option 3) you should also be able to use most of your office applications (word processor, spreadsheet, etc.) and gain access to any important files, though graphics-intensive software like games probably won't work. However, the main purpose of Safe Mode is to track down faults that make Windows crash, or prevent it from loading properly.

If the problem began soon after installing a new item of hardware or software your first port of call should be the Windows Device Manager. Right-click on My Computer and select Properties (or Start > Settings > Control Panel > System), select the Device Manager tab and look for any yellow exclamation marks on the list that appears. These indicate that conflicts have occurred between a new hardware device or program, and it is interfering with your existing configuration. You should be able to resolve it by highlighting the item concerned, click the Properties button, a window will appear with a brief description of the problem and often a possible solution.

Safe Mode is useful for tracking down problems associated with programs that load automatically at the same time as Windows. If you suspect one of them is misbehaving you can remove them one at a time from the Start-up program group (Start > Programs > Start Up) then restart Windows as normal.

Windows 98 and ME have some additional utilities than can help troubleshoot problems if Windows will only load in Safe Mode. Go to Run on the Start menu and type 'msconfig'. This displays all of the main start-up files on a series of tabbed pages, with the option to disable individual entries. There's also a Selective Start-up mode on the General tab that allows you to bypass specified files completely. This is an extremely useful facility and it can be used to solve a great many start-up (and shutdown) problems. While it can be very time consuming, you should be able to isolate the offending file or file entry by a simple process of trial and error. In other words disable one item at a time and re-start the PC. It is vitally important that you only change one item at a time and remember to reinstate each one after every attempt.

LOADING ERRORS AND LOCK-UPS

If Windows loads successfully, but with error messages concerning missing files or drivers, this can often be traced to a recent incomplete uninstallation, especially if you tried to remove a program by deleting it from within Windows Explorer. The name of the missing file should give you a clue to the application. You can re-install the software and then use the program's own uninstaller or Add/Remove programs in Control panel to do the job properly.

Frequent lock-ups can sometimes be resolved from Device Manager by changing the display and hard disk settings. Select the Performance tab, click on the Graphics button and set the 'Hardware Acceleration' slider to none. Select the File System button and set the 'Read Ahead Optimisation' slider to none. Only change one thing at a time though, and re-boot the PC afterwards to see if it has any effect.

Q&A **Real world problems**

Check list

Q   My C:\ drive is overrun by .chk files, amounting to over 200 megabytes which, when opened in Notepad, consist of gibberish with occasional snippets from Help files for a program I uninstalled years ago, and the occasional mention of the words 'Java' and 'Internet'. On a 1.6 gig hard drive, this is space I'd rather not waste. Is it safe to delete these files, or will nasty errors occur?
O.S. via e-mail

A   Lots of *.chk files is a sure sign your PC is crashing or you haven't been shutting it down properly. They are created by Scandisk, which automatically checks the hard disk for errors after Windows or running programs unexpectedly stop running. Most programs – including Windows – create temporary files whilst they are running and they're normally deleted when the program is shut down. Following an improper shutdown Scandisk clears up the clutter left behind on the hard disk drive and converts it to a *.chk file, in case the data is important and you want to retrieve it. If the PC and your applications appear to be running normally then you can safely delete those *.chk files, but the way to avoid creating more of them is to exit Windows properly, or sort out any problems that are causing your machine to crash.

Scan plan

Q   My problem is with Scandisk, both the Standard and Thorough tests. I find that it gets to about 50%, goes back to the beginning and starts again. This is repeated several times. If I let it continue, the following notice appears on the screen: 'Scan Disk has restarted 10 times because Windows, or another program has been writing to the drive'. To my knowledge from looking at the Desktop, no other programs are operating.
F.H. via e-mail

A   There must be one or more programs still running in the background, the most likely ones are a screensaver or a virus scanner. Disable both and if that doesn't work press Crtl + Alt + Delete once, to open the Close Program dialogue box, and use End Task to close everything except Explorer and Systray, then try again. If all else fails you can try the DOS Scandisk utility on your Emergency Start-up disk. Boot up from the disk and type 'Scandisk c:' at the A: prompt and press Enter.

Scan switch

Q   I recently installed a program that interfered with the working of my computer, so I uninstalled it. However, this has had the effect of removing the facility for the computer to run Scandisk on re-starting when it has been switched off after a freeze. How can I get Scandisk to load automatically as it was before?
E.W. Surrey

A   In Windows 98 the option to switch disable Scandisk after a bad shutdown can be found by typing 'msconfig' in Run on the Start menu; select the General tab and click the Advanced button. In Windows 95 you can put a Scandisk shortcut into the Start-up folder and specify when and how it is activated. Full details are in Windows Help, select the Index tab and type Scandisk in the keyword search field.

Bad attitude

Q   I have seen the term 'bad sectors' mentioned on several occasions but it is never fully explained. Can you explain what they are, the cause, and if they show up with Scandisk, whether there is any means of clearing the fault. A friend ran Scandisk on a good computer, which he rarely uses, only to find that it indicated a large number of bad sectors. He ran Scandisk several more times and each run produced substantial increases in the number of bad sectors until about a third of his disk was shown as bad. It was suggested that re-formatting might help. In the end I suggested he continued running his computer, because the large amount of remaining good sectors was adequate for his requirements. In two years, the disk is still in good order and the level of bad sectors has remained constant.

C.H. via e-mail

A A bad sector is an area of the disk that programs like Scandisk determine is not capable of reliably storing data. This can be due to a number of reasons, from defects in the magnetic material coating the disk to mechanical problems with the read/write heads and mechanism. In fact many brand new disk drives have bad sectors but these are detected during manufacture and 'mapped out'. In other words tests show they are not going to get any worse and the rest of the drive functions perfectly well, so the 'firmware' program that controls the drive is programmed not to use those parts of the disk. However, if bad sectors develop subsequently that is a sign of potential trouble. Occasionally the problem stabilises, as in the case of your friend's drive, and sometimes reformatting makes bad sectors disappear, but this may only be temporary. It is sensible to take the appearance of bad sectors as a warning of possible catastrophic failure, backup files and replace the drive as soon as possible. These days hard disk drives are not expensive, but the data they contain can be irreplaceable!

Dilligent defrag

Q I have seen advice that hard drives should be defragged when fragmentation levels reach 8%. This might mean running Defrag preceded by Scandisk every month or so. A local computer technician tells me that fragmentation rapidly reaches the 10% mark then levels off between 10 and 15% and stays at these levels for months. This is quite acceptable, and defrag need not be run more that once a year as the defrag process puts a large strain on the disk drive mechanism. So who is correct? Is defrag a cunning way of drive manufacturers to get us to wear out hard drives quickly, or is the computer technician not the expert he claims to be? How harmful is Scandisk? How

often should a full surface scan be carried out? Definitive advice to the confused please!
G.M. via e-mail

A   Whilst Defrag and to a lesser extent, Scandisk, makes the hard disk drive work a little harder than usual, it's well within normal operating parameters and there is no evidence that it has an impact on a drive's life expectancy. In fact hard disk drives are incredibly reliable and the chances are you will replace your PC long before the drive wears out. The amount of file fragmentation depends entirely on how much use the PC gets, and the type of software you are using. On some heavyweight applications there can be a noticeable reduction in speed when fragmentation reaches just 5%. Running Scandisk and defragging once a month is about right for most home users. You only need to carry out a full surface scan if a routine Scandisk session reports errors, which may indicate that the drive has problems.

CHAPTER 3

Switching off

The last thing you need first thing in the morning is a PC with attitude, telling you that because you didn't shut it down properly last time, you're going to have to wait while it checks your disk drive for errors. Needless to say you would dearly like to shut down your PC properly, but it won't let you, so you have to go through this tiresome ritual, and be cheekily chastised by your PC for something that almost certainly was not your fault . . .

WHEN WINDOWS WON'T GO AWAY . . .

As if getting Windows to boot up doesn't cause enough problems, closing it down afterwards can be a real headache for a lot of PC owners. Faced with a machine that 'hangs' during shutdown most users head straight for the on-off switch but this is really not a good idea. Most of the time, if the machine freezes in the middle of shutdown, you'll get away with switching it off but if the power is cut whilst the PC is in the middle of an operation very bad things might happen. Never switch off if the hard disk activity light is flashing or you can hear the drive chattering; if you do then critical Windows system files might be corrupted and you could be even worse off, with a completely dead machine. Suffice it to say, given the option it is far better to try a few things first, to see if you can shut down your PC in an orderly manner.

In Windows a lot of complicated sounding things need to happen before the 'It is safe. . .' message appears or the machine switches itself off; these include unloading and re-configuring driver files, clearing out or 'flushing' an area of the hard disk drive called a 'cache' of temporary files, completing all disk writing operations and finally closing down programs. Whilst Windows will normally exit running applications automatically some may not respond, so before clicking Shutdown it's always a good idea to check you haven't missed something or that there's nothing happening behind the scenes by making sure the taskbar is clear of icons and pressing Alt + Tab; if nothing appears on the screen you can proceed. If the PC 'hangs' at the 'Please Wait. . .' screen, don't be impatient and switch off, give it a minute or two, especially if the hard disk activity light is still flickering, some programs can take a while to finish what they are doing.

Even if you do everything by the book the most well behaved PCs can still hang from time to time. Usually the worst thing that happens after an aborted shutdown is a brief delay the next time you switch on whilst the Scandisk utility runs through a series of checks on the disk drive, after which Windows loads and shuts down normally again.

However, a small percentage of PCs suffer from persistent shutdown problems. It's not something you should have to put up with and most of the time the solution is fairly simple, usually involving uninstalling a program or changing a setting, but tracking down the original cause can be time-consuming. A lot of shutdown problems can be traced back to the most recent program or piece of hardware that you installed, in which case try uninstalling and re-installing it. If that doesn't work, and your PC is otherwise behaving itself, take the matter up with whoever is responsible for the errant product or visit the company's website and look for the product support or FAQ (frequently asked questions) sections for any mention of conflicts, bugs, or updates that may help.

If shutdown has always been erratic or it started playing up spontaneously you're going to have to do a bit of detective work. There are any number of possible causes so it's a process of elimination. If you have closed all running applications and your PC hangs try pressing Ctrl + Alt + Delete to bring up the Close Program menu to make sure no frozen programs have been left behind. Work your way down the list, highlighting each item in turn and clicking End Task, then try for a shutdown. You can do this for any entry except Explorer and System Tray, which cannot be closed.

It's worth checking for a corrupted sound file so go to Start > Settings > Control Panel > Sounds. Find Exit Windows on the list and change the setting in the Sound Name field to None, then try shutting down again. Your PC's power management system is another potential trouble spot; open Power Management in Control Panel and switch the Power Scheme to Always On and the System and Monitor standby times to Never then see what happens when you shut down.

The next thing to try is to disable all of the programs that load during start-up. To do that, press and hold the Shift key at switch on until after

```
┌─────────────────────────────────────────────────────────┐
│  ⋮ Close Program                                    [X]   │
├─────────────────────────────────────────────────────────┤
│  ┌────────────────────────────────────────────────┬──┐   │
│  │ Dial-up Connection                             │▲ │   │
│  │ Explorer                                       │  │   │
│  │ Date/Time Properties                           │  │   │
│  │ Power Management Properties                    │  │   │
│  │ Sounds Properties                              │  │   │
│  │ Csinsm32                                       │  │   │
│  │ Monwow                                         │  │   │
│  │ Qshlf99z                                       │  │   │
│  │ Quickres                                       │  │   │
│  │ Systray                                        │▼ │   │
│  │ ◄                                            ► │  │   │
│  └────────────────────────────────────────────────┴──┘   │
│                                                           │
│  WARNING: Pressing CTRL+ALT+DEL again will restart your   │
│  computer. You will lose unsaved information in all       │
│  programs that are running.                               │
│                                                           │
│  ┌──────────────┐  ┌──────────────┐  ┌──────────────┐     │
│  │   End Task   │  │  Shut Down   │  │    Cancel    │     │
│  └──────────────┘  └──────────────┘  └──────────────┘     │
└─────────────────────────────────────────────────────────┘
```

Pressing Ctrl + Alt + Delete brings up the Close
Program dialogue box, to show you what programs
are still running

Windows has finished loading. Windows 95 machines will boot up in Safe Mode (see Chapter 2), Windows 98 and ME load more or less normally but you'll notice that there are no programs shown on the taskbar or System Tray. Now shut the PC down, if it obliges then you know that one of the programs in the start-up group is to blame.

On a Windows 95 PC open Start Up (Start > Programs > Start Up) and remove the programs one by one by right-clicking on the icons and selecting Delete, then re-boot the PC each time, until normal operation is restored. Windows 98 and ME have a useful tool called 'Msconfig' which can help identify and troubleshoot a lot of shutdown problems. Go to Run on the Start menu and type msconfig, and select the General tab. Check the item 'Selective Startup' uncheck Process System.ini file, click OK, shut down, boot up and try shutting down again. Do the same with the Win.Ini file. If that doesn't help select the Startup tab in msconfig and disable the programs

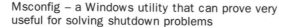

Msconfig – a Windows utility that can prove very
useful for solving shutdown problems

that Windows loads automatically one by one, trying for a clean shutdown
each time. The last thing to try is select the General tab, click the Advanced
button and check the item 'Disable Fast Shutdown'. If none of the above
works don't forget to return all settings back to the original or default values.

The complex Windows filing system has been know to cause its fair share
of problems. There's an easy way to find out if this is the cause: go to
Control Panel, double click the System icon, select Performance, the File
System button and the Troubleshooting tab. Put a check in all of the boxes,
click OK, close Control Panel and shut down Windows. If it is successful go
back and uncheck the items one at a time.

Corrupt Windows device drivers can trigger all sorts of odd behaviour; if
all else has failed so far double click on the System icon in Control Panel and

select the Device Manager tab. Anything listed with an exclamation mark in a yellow circle next to it is worth investigating. Double click on the suspect item (or right click and choose Properties) and check the box marked 'Disable in this hardware profile' and try shutting the PC down. Don't forget to restore the original setting afterwards and only try it on one item at a time. If a driver turns out to be the source of the problem use System Properties to remove it, but before you do make sure you have the original driver disk to hand.

Advanced Power Management is another area to check. In Control Panel click on the System icon, then the Device Manager tab and click the '+' sign next to System Devices, select Advanced Power Management and if it has been enabled, check the 'Disable in this profile' option, click OK, exit Control Panel and attempt a restart and shutdown. If that doesn't work go back to Control Panel click on the Power Management and on the Power Schemes tab, under Power Schemes, select Always On and see if that makes a difference.

That covers the most common shutdown problems that users can safely tackle by themselves, but there's plenty more to try, if you know your way around Windows. There's a useful set of 'Troubleshooters' on the Microsoft website, that take you through the investigative process, step by step. The addresses for each version of Windows are:

- Windows 95: http://support.microsoft.com/support/kb/articles/Q145/9/26.asp
- Windows 98: http://support.microsoft.com/support/kb/articles/Q202/6/33.ASP
- Windows 98 SE: http://support.microsoft.com/support/kb/articles/Q238/0/96.ASP
- Windows ME: http://support.microsoft.com/support/kb/articles/Q273/7/46.ASP

Shutdown problems concerning other Microsoft applications can be found at: http://support.microsoft.com/support/tshoot/default.asp

Q&A   **Real world problems**

Faster exit

Q   I have recently started using Windows 98 and one of the little irritations that I have come across is having to press 'Start' on the task bar in order to shut down. Is there a way of putting a shortcut icon for shutting down on the desktop?
J.G. via e-mail

A   Yes there is, just follow these instructions. Right–click into an empty area of the desktop; select New and then Shortcut from the Menu. The create shortcut wizard starts and in the Command Line box type: 'c:\windows\ rundll.exe user.exe,exitwindows' (omitting the quote marks of course, and watch the punctuation and spaces). Click Next, clear the name box and type in your own name for the shortcut, something like Quick Exit, then click Finish. Incidentally, there are also keyboard shortcuts Alt + F4 and Win key + U, which respectively close open applications and get you to the Windows Shut Down menu. There are also third–party applications, which will do the job, such as Exits95 (which also works with Win98) which can be downloaded from: http://petervw.club.tip.nl

Shutdown stalls

Q.   I have Windows ME and when I select 'Shut Down' from the start menu, the monitor goes off, but the processor unit stays on. I have to disconnect it from the mains. Any suggestions?
R.G. via e-mail

A   This is almost certainly a Power Management problem. Try this: right click on My Computer and select Properties then the Device Manager tab. Scroll down the list and click on the plus sign next to System Devices, click and highlight Advanced Power Management, then Properties and the Settings tab and check the item 'Force APM mode'. If that doesn't help there's a comprehensive Windows ME shutdown 'troubleshooter' article on the Microsoft website at: http://support.microsoft.com/support/kb/articles/ Q273/7/46.ASP

Hot metal

Q I have an old office computer, which was upgraded having a new hard drive and new CD-ROM drive fitted. It works perfectly but for one thing. After I have been using it for about one hour a bleeping sound starts. I think it may be overheating but moving it to cooler places does not seem to work. To get rid of the sound I have to turn the computer off each time and wait for half an hour before I can use it again. Please help as I have to write long essays on it and it takes forever!
M.R. via e-mail

A It certainly sounds like a thermal problem. It could be that adding the CD-ROM drive and new hard disk drive has put a strain on the PC's power supply, causing it to overheat; though that wouldn't explain the 'bleeping' sound. It's more likely that the CPU is running hot. Virtually all Pentium PCs and many 486 models have small cooling fans and finned metal heat sinks mounted on the microprocessor chip. These fans can and do fail – sometimes quite noisily – allowing the chip to overheat. It could be that the fan wasn't re-connected or the wiring was disturbed when the new drives were fitted. The only way to check is to remove the lid and see if the fan is running when the PC is switched on. They're not expensive (£5 to £10) and normally quite easy to replace – most just clip on – but if you don't feel up to the job, or the fan is working then the machine will need to be looked at by an engineer.

Closure crash

Q I have a Windows 98 PC with Office 2000 software. When I try to close down a message appears on screen saying a 'Fatal exception OE has occurred at 0028:c16000A3 . . . it may be possible for you to continue, press any key to continue'. When a key is pressed the PC freezes and I have to switch it off. I have had everything reinstalled on my PC and the hardware checked but to no avail. Can you suggest a cause?
H.S. via e-mail

A Fatal exception errors are often hardware related and more often than not are caused by faulty RAM memory cards. Sometimes it is possible to resolve the problem by changing BIOS settings but it's usually easier and quicker to replace the errant module. It's not a difficult job, but it's not something you should tackle yourself if you've never delved into the innards of your PC.

Sticky shut down

Q My PC will not shut down from Windows 95 and freezes on the Windows cloudy sky screen. It then has to be shut down by switching off and consequently needs to do a scan each time it is re-started. Can you help?
G. S. via e-mail

A There are many possible causes, some of them requiring major surgery, but quite often it's something fairly straightforward like a program running in the background not shutting down properly. Try this: before you exit Windows check that the taskbar at the bottom of the screen is clear – i.e. there are no programs or applications still running – then press Ctrl + Alt + Delete just once, and you'll see the Close Program Window. Highlight and click End Task for each entry in turn (except Explorer and System Tray) then exit Windows. If the machine shuts down successfully you'll have to go through the list in Close Program, one by one, to find which one is causing your machine to hang.

Health monitor

Q I use the energy saving function on my PC to switch my monitor off after ten minutes of inactivity. I wonder if potential savings would be more than offset if the monitor needed replacing due to the constant switching on and off.
L. W. via e-mail

A PC monitors are surprisingly robust and most will usually outlast the PCs they're supplied with, so you needn't worry too much about premature ageing. Energy saving systems reduce the strain on critical components, such as the picture tube and power supply, even so if your monitor is being switched on and off more than three or four times a day, say, then you should increase the delay time or adjust your working patterns.

CHAPTER 4

DOS to the rescue

*If you purchased your Windows PC within the last
five years and have no particular interest in games
or specialist applications the chances are that you
have had little or nothing to do with DOS, apart from
that brief flash of text when you switch on your PC
and the occasional (or possibly not so occasional)
mysterious error messages. DOS, or to give it its full
name the Microsoft Disk Operating System (MS-
DOS), is well worth getting to know because one
day it could save your bacon!*

BEHIND THE SCENES

DOS exists mainly in the background on a Windows 95/98 PC, and is more
or less absent from Windows ME, though it can be summoned in an
emergency. Its importance has gradually diminished with each subsequent
release; nevertheless, it can provide a lifeline to revive your PC and recover
data after a nasty crash or when Windows refuses to load. An understanding
of DOS will also help you weave your way through some of the more
puzzling aspects of Windows, so we'll begin with a brief but essential
tutorial on how DOS manages files, then we'll delve a little deeper into its
inner workings and some of the useful things it can do for you.

In Windows 95 and 98 DOS files are loaded from the hard disk into the
PC's memory immediately after the first Windows screen flashes up during
the boot up process. The most important ones are 'msdos.sys', 'io.sys',
'autoexec.bat' and 'config.sys'. Between them they tell the PC about the
devices and peripherals connected to the machine, and the software it is
using. Then it's on to stage three, DOS is shunted to the sidelines as
Windows loads and takes command of the PC.

Windows now becomes the PC's primary operating system; it controls
how the computer's hardware and software communicates and interacts and

presents you with the Graphical User Interface (GUI or 'gooey'). This is the familiar Windows 'desktop'. Essentially DOS does the same job but without all the frills and pretty graphics; instead of clicking on icons things are made to happen by typing in text commands and keyboard actions. DOS interprets the commands and turns them into a language the computer understands, called machine code.

Because DOS uses text-based instructions and doesn't need layers of extra software for colourful graphics, it is much simpler than Windows. It is also a lot faster, which is why until recently most of the best computer games were DOS-based, though with the advent of faster processors, larger disk drives, increased memory capacity and more advanced graphics controllers most recent fast action games work within Windows.

There are two ways to get into DOS on Windows 95 and 98 PCs. You can stop Windows from loading during the boot up sequence (see Chapter 2) or you can start a DOS 'session' within Windows that allows you to peek inside DOS. To do that click on the MS-DOS Prompt icon in Start > Programs. This loads a program called Command.com, a black window opens on the screen and you will see a Microsoft copyright message and below that a line that reads: C:\Windows>, followed by a flashing cursor. This line is known as the Command Prompt and it tells you a number of things. C: is the identification letter assigned to your PC's main hard disk drive, backslash Windows (\Windows) shows the directory your PC is currently using, and the greater than symbol and cursor (>_) indicates DOS is ready and waiting for an instruction or command. Now type in the command 'dir' (without the quotation marks), a long list of file names will flash past on the screen and the command prompt appears at the bottom of the screen once again. The command 'dir' is short for Directory, it instructs the computer to show the contents of the Windows directory.

At this stage it's wise to look but not touch; DOS is extremely powerful, a few careless keystrokes can wreak havoc, so close the window in the usual way, by clicking on the 'X' icon in the top right-hand corner. If you're feeling bold, type the command 'exit' (without the quotation marks) and the window disappears.

This brief encounter with DOS illustrates how information is organised on your PC's hard disk. The disk drive is like a filing cabinet containing thousands of files – the basic storage unit for data and programs. Related files are collected together into folders, directories and subdirectories (folders within folders). There is one exception to this rule and that is the 'root

```
MS-DOS Prompt                                                    _ B x
T 13 x 22    □ ▣ ▣ ⊠ ⌂ A
(continuing C:\WINDOWS)
BCD       INI            0  23/02/00  14:06  BCD.INI
BCDSETUP  LOG            0  23/02/00  14:02  BcdSetup.log
BINDLI~1  TXT       19,600  25/12/99  21:14  Bind List Log.txt
BLACKT~1  BMP          182  11/05/98  20:01  Black Thatch.bmp
BLUERI~1  BMP          194  11/05/98  20:01  Blue Rivets.bmp
BRNDLOG   TXT        4,282  09/01/00  20:29  brndlog.txt
BRNDLOG   BAK       15,041  25/12/99  17:43  brndlog.bak
BUBBLES   BMP        2,118  11/05/98  20:01  Bubbles.bmp
CALC      EXE       94,208  11/05/98  20:01  CALC.EXE
CARVED~1  BMP          582  11/05/98  20:01  Carved Stone.bmp
CATROOT        <DIR>       01/08/99  20:36  CATROOT
CD32      EXE      799,487  20/05/99  10:35  cd32.exe
CDPLAYER  EXE      106,496  11/05/98  20:01  CDPLAYER.EXE
CHANNE~1  SCR       91,888  25/12/99  21:13  Channel Screen Saver.SCR
CIRCLES   BMP          190  11/05/98  20:01  Circles.bmp
CLEANMGR  EXE      131,072  11/05/98  20:01  CLEANMGR.EXE
CLOUD     GIF       11,306  11/05/98  20:01  CLOUD.GIF
CLSPACK   EXE       49,424  25/01/99  10:09  CLSPACK.EXE
CMD640X   SYS       24,626  11/05/98  20:01  CMD640X.SYS
CMD640X2  SYS       20,901  11/05/98  20:01  CMD640X2.SYS
COHKB     DRV        1,474  15/02/00  17:01  cohkb.drv
COMMAND        <DIR>       01/08/99  20:35  COMMAND
Press any key to continue . . .
```

Typing Dir at the DOS command lists the contents of a
directory, in this case the Windows folder

directory' mentioned earlier. This is a special section of the hard disk
(represented by the backslash after the C prompt (i.e. C:\)). The root
directory is set aside for important systems files and directories that the PC
accesses when it first boots up, and this is where the DOS files live. In other
words – and this is the key point – you can load DOS, and from there gain
access to any other directory on the hard disk, without Windows – that's
what makes it so useful!

HOW TO RETRIEVE IMPORTANT FILES

Now that you know what DOS looks like it's time to look at some basic
commands and how they can get you out of a fix following a fatal
Windows crash. In this case you have no option but to start your PC in
DOS mode, either by using your emergency start-up disk (all versions)
or by starting the PC in Safe Mode (Windows 95 and 98 only) and
selecting Command Prompt from the list of options. To start in Safe Mode
switch on, wait a few moments for it to complete the POST (power on
self-test) sequence, then before the 'Starting Windows . . .' message appears
press the F8 key.

When starting in DOS mode you will see a black screen with a command line prompt with either drive A: or drive C: selected. You can change disk drives by typing the drive letter, followed by a colon, thus to change from floppy drive A, to drive C type C: and press the Return key. You may or may not be able to access your PC's CD-ROM drive (usually drive D:) depending upon whether or not the appropriate DOS driver has been loaded, or you started the PC using the Windows 98 or ME start-up disk. To exit from DOS mode (provided no programs are running) just switch the PC off, or type 'win', which will load Windows.

The C:\> prompt shows that you are in the 'root directory' of your PC's hard disk drive, which contains the important system files that configure the machine during boot up, and all of the folders or directories containing Windows and the programs loaded on your PC, though if your hard disk has been split, its 'partitioned' data and software may be on a virtual 'D:' drive. The root of the C: drive is not a very interesting place so we'll use the change directory command to have a peek inside the Windows folder on the C: drive. Type cd\windows and Return and the command prompt changes to C:\WINDOWS>, showing that we are now inside the Windows folder; 'cd' stands for change directory, and that kind of logical simplicity holds true for most DOS commands; note also that you can use upper or lowercase for DOS commands and filenames.

Now we can use the dir (directory) command, which tells the PC to display the contents of the current directory. Type it in and see what happens. A long list of files and folders flashes past and you probably won't see much but you can tell DOS to display only one page at a time by adding a 'switch' to the command, in this case /p (p for page) so this time type dir /p and Return. You can also list the contents of the directory alphabetically, by date, size and many other ways by adding a sort switch /o (sOrt) followed by a second letter that tells DOS how to arrange the list. For example, to list the files one page at a time in date order the command would be dir /p /od, to list in order of size use the sort command switch /os, for an alphabetical listing use /on, and so on.

You may have noticed that file and folder names in DOS are only 8 characters long; DOS shortens the longer file names used in Windows to the first six characters followed by a tilde (~) and a number (normally 1, unless there's another file with the same first six letters). When naming files you should use the DOS convention, i.e. as it appears on the screen.

You should now have enough information to be able to navigate your way around your PC's disk drives, so let's put that knowledge to some practical use

```
MS-DOS Prompt
13 x 22
SCANDISK  LOG              4,628   21/02/00   17:56  SCANDISK.LOG
TBRIDGE          <DIR>              27/12/99   12:49  TBRIDGE
BACKUP           <DIR>              11/09/99    9:21  backup
QUICKENW         <DIR>              08/10/99   22:43  quickenw
OUTLOO~1         <DIR>              15/10/99   20:14  Outlook Express
POWERT~1         <DIR>              21/12/99   18:56  powertoys
DOWNLO~1         <DIR>              22/12/99   12:26  downloads
SETUPXLG  TXT              454      09/01/00   20:29  SETUPXLG.TXT
READIRIS         <DIR>              27/12/99   12:51  READIRIS
ACROREAD         <DIR>              27/12/99   12:52  ACROREAD
MAILSAFE         <DIR>              25/12/99    9:25  Mailsafe
TESTCA~1         <DIR>              22/12/99    9:33  Testcards
ZIPPERS          <DIR>              07/01/00   15:18  Zippers
WINDOW~1  BMK              63       16/01/00   20:06  WINDOWSWinHlp32.BMK
CONFIG    SYS             102       28/01/00   23:19  CONFIG.SYS
AUTOEXEC  BAT             200       27/01/00   12:01  AUTOEXEC.BAT
LIPREFS   JS              151       07/02/00   14:05  liprefs.js
MYMUSI~1         <DIR>              14/02/00   14:21  My Music
MP3TRA~1         <DIR>              15/02/00   16:30  MP3 tracks
          10 file(s)         107,788 bytes
          19 dir(s)        1,882.04 MB free

C:\>cd\mydocu~1

C:\My Documents>_
```

DOS file names can only be eight characters long; note the use
of the tilde (~) to denote long file names

with a simple exercise. We are going to use the DOS Copy command to recover an important document by copying it to a floppy disk. If you want to follow this example use Windows Explorer to open My Documents, go to New on the File menu to create a new subfolder, rename it Office then use your word processor to save a text file into the new folder and call it 'meetings.doc'. Boot the PC to DOS mode: in a real life situation that would probably mean using your emergency recovery disk; if you use that method don't forget to change the drive letter from A: to C:, remove the disk from the drive and insert a blank formatted floppy. When using the Copy command DOS needs to know three things: the name of the folder or subfolders the document is in – also known as the 'path' – the name of the document or file and where you want it to go. If you use file names of more than 8 characters remember those tildes and numbers. Thus the DOS command to copy our important document from the hard disk to a floppy disk would be:

'copy c:\mydocu~1\office\meetings.doc a:'

It probably looks more complicated than it is but try it a couple of times with your own folders and documents and you'll soon get the hang of it.

```
MS-DOS Prompt                                                          _ | 6 | X
T 13 x 22 ▾  ☐ ▭ ▣ ⊠ ☗ ☐ A
TBRIDGE         <DIR>           27/12/99   12:49  TBRIDGE
BACKUP          <DIR>           11/09/99    9:21  backup
QUICKENW        <DIR>           08/10/99   22:43  quickenw
OUTLOO~1        <DIR>           15/10/99   20:14  Outlook Express
POWERT~1        <DIR>           21/12/99   18:56  powertoys
DOWNLO~1        <DIR>           22/12/99   12:26  downloads
SETUPXLG TXT            454     09/01/00   20:29  SETUPXLG.TXT        ·
READIRIS        <DIR>           27/12/99   12:51  READIRIS
ACROREAD        <DIR>           27/12/99   12:52  ACROREAD
MAILSAFE        <DIR>           25/12/99    9:25  Mailsafe
TESTCA~1        <DIR>           22/12/99    9:33  Testcards
ZIPPERS         <DIR>           07/01/00   15:18  Zippers
WINDOW~1 BMK            63      16/01/00   20:06  WINDOWSWinHlp32.BMK
CONFIG   SYS           102      28/01/00   23:19  CONFIG.SYS
AUTOEXEC BAT           200      27/01/00   12:01  AUTOEXEC.BAT
LIPREFS  JS            151      07/02/00   14:05  liprefs.js
MYMUSI~1        <DIR>           14/02/00   14:21  My Music
MP3TRA~1        <DIR>           15/02/00   16:30  MP3 tracks
          10 file(s)         107,788 bytes
          19 dir(s)        1,881.73 MB free

C:\>copy c:\mydocu~1\office\meetings.doc a:
          1 file(s) copied

C:\>
```

Using the DOS copy command to retrieve important files from a 'dead' PC

ADVANCED COMMANDS

We'll round off this introduction to DOS with a look at some of the more powerful commands and conventions that could come in handy one day if your PC starts misbehaving.

Don't try any of these examples unless you are confident of your abilities. If you are unsure then stay well away from the PC's hard disk (C: drive) and confine your experiments to a floppy disk in drive A: prepare one beforehand by using Windows Explorer to copy a few documents and text files to a floppy.

Boot up your PC or exit Windows to the DOS mode and change to drive letter A by typing A: at the C:> (or C:\Windows >) prompt. DOS has a Help facility; it's quite crude by comparison with Windows Help and earlier versions of DOS (prior to Windows 95) but it is very easy to use. Simply type in the command after the flashing A: or C: prompt, followed by the switch '/?' (as usual without the inverted commas). For example, to find out how the change directory (cd) command works, and how to use it type 'cd /?' and press Return.

Locating files and folders in DOS (and Windows) can be made a lot easier by the use of 'Wildcards'. A wildcard represents an unspecified character or characters. The two wildcards used in DOS are the asterisk '*', which can mean literally anything, from a single character to a whole filename; the other one is the question mark '?', which represents a single character only. For example, if you wanted to tell the PC to list just the document files in a particular directory you would use the command 'dir *.doc', where the asterisk represents all files with the extension .doc. You could use the '?' wildcard to limit a directory search to a group of files with a four letter filename thus: 'dir ????.doc'.

When moving files around on your PC it's useful to be able to create a new directory on a hard or floppy disk drive: for that you need the MD (Make Directory) command. This is similar to 'New' on the File menu in Windows Explorer. If you want to create a new directory called 'office' just type md, followed by a backslash and the name of the new directory, thus: 'md\office'. To create a new directory on another disk drive – e.g. hard drive C, insert the drive letter, followed by a colon, into the command, so from the A:> prompt you would type 'md c:\office'.

You can copy the entire contents of one disk to another using a DOS utility called Diskcopy. To duplicate a floppy disk, for example, the command would read 'discopy a: a:'. If you're wondering how that works when you only have one floppy disk drive, DOS first reads the contents of the source disk into the PC's memory, prompts you to load a fresh floppy, onto which it writes the files.

It's possible to change filenames and extensions using the Rename command, usually shortened to just 'ren'. To rename a file called 'meetings.doc' to 'calendar.doc', type the command 'ren meetings.doc calendar.doc' and it's done. By now your monitor is probably looking a bit crowded so here's a quick and simple way to get rid of the clutter: type 'cls' (Clear Screen) at the A: prompt to empty the screen. Whilst we're at it, here's another quick one, type 'mem' and you'll see a full breakdown of your PC's memory configuration.

DOS can display the contents of any file using the command 'Type', but this will not allow you to change its contents and in any case you won't be able to see it all, if it fills more than a single screen. However, DOS also includes a full screen text editor, called 'Edit', that will allow you to change, save and print the contents of a file. Type 'edit' at the command prompt the screen turns blue, and a Windows type menu bar appears at the top. You can also open a file directly by adding the name of the file after the edit command, i.e. 'edit meetings.doc'. Note that if you open a non-ASCII text file or a formatted document, created in a word processor like Word, the file will contain lots of gobbledegook characters and symbols. Whilst the PC is in DOS mode you will probably find that your mouse doesn't work; this is quite normal if a DOS mouse driver hasn't been installed. To use Edit you'll have to resort to the keyboard, press ALT to highlight the first menu item, use the right and left cursor arrow keys to change menu items, and the up/down arrows to select commands.

Finally some heavy-duty commands that you should treat with great caution. You can erase entire directories with the 'rd' (Remove Directory) command. To erase the office directory you have created the command would be 'rd a:\office'. Be warned, there are no undo facilities or a Recycle Bin in DOS; when it's gone it's gone! To remove individual files you can use the 'del' (Delete) command and this is also very powerful since you can use it with wildcards to erase whole groups of files. For example, to delete all of the document files within a folder, use cd to change to the folder's directory and type 'del *.doc /p', the /p switch is important as it will ask you to confirm each deletion.

That's just a quick taste of what DOS can do, if you would like to find out more the latest revision of the classic 'DOS For Dummies' is well worth reading and there are plenty of websites to peruse, including:

http://www.computerhope.com/msdos.htm

Q&A Real world problems

DOS help

Q Where can I find a list of the available DOS commands? Help is only of help if you already know what the command is. There must be a list hidden away somewhere in the system!
W.W. via e-mail

A There used to be on earlier versions of MS-DOS but a lot of useful things like that were stripped out when DOS was integrated into Windows 95.

However, you'll find a complete list of commands, what they do and how to use them at:

http://www.easydos.com/dosindex.html

Drive off

Q I have a Windows 98 PC with DVD-ROM and Zip drives. The drives are available to me in Windows but not in DOS. I would like to be able to access the DVD drive from DOS when playing some of my older games on CD-ROM but it says that there is no DVD drive when I try.
T.C. via e-mail

A DVD-ROM and Zip drives will only work if the relevant DOS driver software has been installed. The driver disks should have been supplied with your PC: if not you should contact the supplier, installation instructions are normally contained in a 'readme' text file. Driver software can also be downloaded from the Internet, but you will need to know the make and model number of your DVD-ROM.

Failed format

Q I decided to bite the bullet and format my hard drive. All went well up to the warning and question 'Proceed with Format (Y/N)?' After typing 'Y' the system swung into action, for about three seconds and then came up with the message 'Insufficient memory to transfer system files. Format terminated'. I thought the idea was to delete all the files so that I would have a shiny, clean hard drive. Your help would be appreciated.
A.T. via e-mail

A Assuming that you have booted your PC to the DOS command prompt using the Start-up disk, try changing the drive letter from A: to C:, and then type the format command, i.e. 'C:\ format C: /s'.

Clean machine

Q When one buys or inherits a computer from someone else, which has been used extensively by them, could you recommend a series of actions to 'cleanup' the machine? For example, what is the safest and quickest way to clear out old files, documents, games, unwanted programs, etc. What is the minimum 'clean' configuration to end up with almost as if one had just purchased it from a retailer?

G.B. via e-mail

A   Strictly speaking, unless all of the rights and licences to the software on a 'used' PC, along with the original program disks, are transferred to the new owner then the disk drive should be wiped clean. This is advisable in any case, if only from the standpoint of security, and saving the seller from any comebacks if there are any software problems. To do that boot the PC using an Emergency Recovery Disk and at the A:\ prompt use the 'fdisk c:' followed by the 'format c:' commands to clear the disk and prepare it for the next owner.

Quick DOS

Q   Is there an easy way to start my PC in DOS mode, apart from using the Start-up disk, or starting the PC in Safe Mode, which I find difficult as you have to press the F8 key at exactly the right moment?

J.L. via e-mail

A   You can easily modify one of your PC's start-up files to do this. Use Notepad (Start > Programs > Accessories) to open 'msdos.sys' in the root directory of your C: drive and look for the line BootGUI=1, change that to BootGUI=0, save and close and Windows will now boot to the C: prompt. To start Windows just type 'win'. (You may have to uncheck its Read Only attribute by right clicking on the msdos.sys file icon in Windows Explorer).

Latent logo

Q   After upgrading to Windows 98 my PC still shows the Windows 95 logo on start up. How can one change that? I am loath to reload the Windows installation CD unless absolutely necessary.

F.C. via e-mail

A   You can disable the start-up logo by adding or changing a command in the msdos.sys file, or you can delete or change the opening graphic, which is called logo.sys; both files are stored in the root directory of your C: drive. First open Windows Explorer, highlight drive C: go to the View menu then Folder Options, choose the View tab and in the Advanced Settings Window check the item Show All files. To disable the opening screen right-click on msdos.sys, choose properties and deselect Read Only under Attributes, now open Notepad (Start > Programs > Accessories) and open msdos.sys, under Options change the line Logo=1 to Logo=0, or enter the line if it's not there. Select Save on the File menu and don't forget to change the Attribute back to Read Only when you have finished.

Master plan

Q   I have a Pentium machine with Windows 98 operating system. I have been continuously upgrading the computer and as it started with a 500-Mb hard drive I upgraded this by adding an 8 GB hard drive. I didn't want to have to bother with reconfiguring the whole system so I put the new drive in as a slave D:\ drive. The only problem is that everything wants to install to the C:\ drive, which after Windows 98 and drivers has no space on it. How can I tell Windows to use the D:\ drive as the default drive, or could I change the letter designation of the drives so that it boots from the D:\ drive and has the 8 GB C:\ as the slave?
Ritchie Wilkinson, ritchiewilkinson@hotmail.com

A   The quickest and simplest solution would be to make Drive D bootable, install Windows 98 on it and then use it as your C: drive. If you haven't already done so make an Emergency Start-up disk from the utility in Add/Remove programs in Control Panel then copy across all the files from the floppy to the root directory of your D: drive. Switch off, open up your PC (observing all the usual precautions) disconnect the data and power cables to the C: drive and change the jumper setting on the D: drive to Master. Remove the Start-up disk and the PC should boot up to a DOS prompt on the C: drive (previously the D: drive). You can now install Windows 98 by changing the drive letter to that of your CD-ROM drive containing your Windows installation disk. When it has finished you can reconnect the old C: drive, configure it as a slave and copy across any files you want to keep. You may find that some previously installed applications on the newly designated C: drive may object to the change, in which case they may have to be reinstalled.

CHAPTER 5

Error messages and how to avoid them

The trouble with Windows error messages is that there are so many of them and they never say anything even vaguely reassuring, like 'don't worry, just do this or that and it'll be alright'. Error messages are either totally incomprehensible or littered with scary words like fatal, invalid, illegal, corrupt, failure and missing . . .

DECIPHERING ERROR MESSAGES

In spite of what you may think, relatively few PC problems are random or spontaneous and taking a few simple precautions can prevent most of them. Error messages tend to fall into one of four basic categories: missing or damaged files, programs or Windows freezing, Windows or other programs doing something they shouldn't and hardware faults. For all Windows related error messages your first port of call should be the 'Knowledge Base' on the Microsoft website, full details of how to access it can be found in Chapter 11. Windows 98 and ME users should definitely pay a visit to the Microsoft Error Message Resource Centre on the web at:

http://support.microsoft.com/support/windows/topics/errormsg/emresctr.asp

The majority of error messages can usually be traced back to a deleted file or new software and hardware installations. The fault may not show up at the time but the next time you start up Windows, it looks for a file or application that isn't there any longer.

Missing Shortcut message boxes (the ones with a waving torch) appear when Windows is loading and they are fairly easy to deal with. They indicate that a program has been improperly deleted and is still listed somewhere, usually in the Start-up folder or one of the Windows system

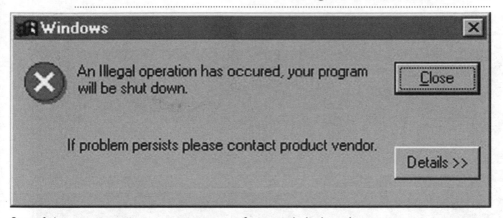

One of the commonest error messages; unfortunately it doesn't
tell you much

files. Go to the Start button then Programs and locate the Start-up folder,
right-click the folder icon, select Open then highlight and delete the
offending item. If that doesn't work try re-installing the missing program
then delete it again, this time using the program's own uninstaller,
Windows Add/Remove program utility in Control Panel or a proprietary
uninstaller program (more about those in a moment).

Incorrect or missing Dynamic Link Library files (DLLs) is another
frequent source of trouble. DLL error messages often appear after installing
or removing programs and the solution is to re-install the offending
software, but this time look for dialogue boxes saying that the files being
loaded are newer or older than the ones currently in use. Check to see if any
of those mentioned are the same as that which appeared in the original error
message and choose the option to load it or replace it, as appropriate. You
can use a similar technique to troubleshoot error messages concerning
missing or corrupt device drivers.

General Protection Fault (GPF) error messages can occur when a
program has a problem with memory resources. The only thing you can
do is close it down by pressing Ctrl + Alt + Delete and select End Task on
the Close Program dialogue box. If you can, save any open files and re-start
the computer. If Windows stopped as well you'll have to re-boot by
pressing Ctrl + Alt + Delete a second time or if that doesn't work, press the
Reset button.

The blue screen 'Fatal Exception' error message (aka the 'blue screen of
death') is a sign that a program has attempted to carry out an illegal

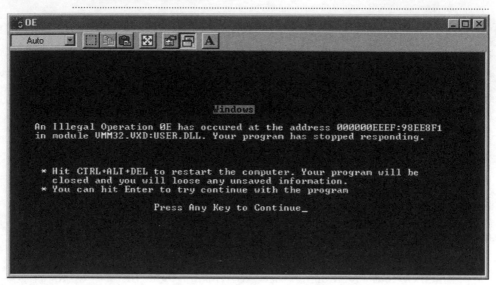

The dreaded 'Blue Screen of Death'

operation. It may help to know what led up to the crash. It could be a combination of keystrokes, opening a particular file, or maybe it only happens when another program is running. Try re-installing the program and if it keeps happening contact the software company to see if there's a known bug or fix available.

Following a Fatal Exception error and GPF, Windows 98, ME and later versions of Windows 95 will usually run the Scandisk utility to check for errors on the hard disk. Occasionally, if the fault is deep-seated, Windows will restart in the Safe Mode (see Chapter 2) loading only the bare minimum of drivers and system files; consequently the screen will usually be in a much lower resolution. Don't worry if this happens, just wait for it to finish loading then shut down; hopefully Windows should restart as normal, though you may have to reset your desktop display options (Start > Settings Taskbar & Start Menu).

Hardware faults are relatively rare and usually the culprit is fairly obvious, it's the device or component you are installing. Very occasionally faults can have a cascade effect and damage the motherboard or processor but in any event there's little you can do, other than replace the part concerned or have the PC looked at by an expert.

The root cause of many error messages is a cluttered hard disk. Every time you install a program dozens of files will be created, some of them ending up inside critical areas of your PC's operating system. Even if you delete the program lots of those files can be left behind. Most lay dormant but it only takes one minor conflict to bring the whole system down. You should install at least one PC housekeeping program. Applications like First Aid and Norton CrashGuard intercept crashes and conflicts before they can do any real damage, allow you to save open files help you to pinpoint the cause and suggest remedies. It's better not to take chances and as soon as possible after you've bought a new PC or re-installed Windows, load a housekeeping utility like Clean Sweep and Uninstaller. These programs monitor every new program you put onto your PC, so that when the time comes they can be cleanly removed. They will also look for orphans, clutter, duplicate files and programs you no longer use, offer to remove them or make compressed backups, until you are ready to delete them permanently. Never install or remove more than one program at a time and afterwards always re-boot the PC and watch for unexpected displays or error messages.

Without any doubt whatsoever the number one cause of PC problems is the user not reading the instructions when installing a piece of hardware or software. We're all guilty as anyone but there is a solution. Take a Post-It note, write on it in very large letters 'RTFM' and stick it to the front of your PC. RTFM is what service engineers mutter under their breath when confronted with faults that wouldn't have happened if the user had bothered to READ THE FLIPPING MANUAL (or words to that effect . . .).

As you add and delete software the structure of the filing system on your PC's hard disk drive becomes disorganised or 'fragmented'. Eventually it can lead to files being lost or corrupted but long before that happens the time it takes for your PC to access information will increase as the read–write heads in the drive search for bits of files spread about your disk drive. This also increases the rate of wear and tear on mechanical components. Defragging your PC on a weekly or monthly basis, depending on whether you are a light or moderate user, will keep your computer's filing system in good order. There are several versions of the Defrag program, depending on which Windows you are using. In Windows 98 there are two, the one in Start > Programs > Accessories > System Tools is the best because it has the option to organise files according to how often they are used, which helps speed up access times. The other one, which is launched by right clicking on the drive icon in My Computer and selecting Properties > Tools works well and is usually a little quicker. You should also run Scandisk before Defrag (also in System Tools and under Tools in My Computer);

every few months use the 'Thorough' option, but leave yourself plenty of time as it can take several hours. If at any time Scandisk finds any errors or bad sectors take that as a timely warning that your disk drive could fail and it is time to get it replaced.

MORE TOP TIPS TO AVOID SEEING ERROR MESSAGES

- Write down error messages, it could help you to track down errant files or assist with calls to technical support helplines
- Never remove programs by deleting folders in Windows Explorer
- When you delete a program or file wait a few days before emptying the Recycle Bin
- Always keep original program and hardware driver disks in a safe place
- Avoid installing unnecessary programs, especially game demos and PC magazine freebies
- Only install one new item of hardware or software at a time
- Make frequent backups of files you are working on – every few minutes if they're really important!

HARDWARE PRECAUTIONS

The PC that doesn't go wrong hasn't been invented – and by the way, that includes the holy Apple Mac. In fact modern PCs are amazingly reliable, considering how complicated they are and component failures are thankfully quite rare. Most hardware faults are avoidable and caused by clumsily installed peripherals, the owner having a fiddle, physical shock and very occasionally high voltage 'spikes' on the mains power supply or telephone line, frying delicate microchips.

Hardware faults are almost impossible to prevent but you can greatly reduce the chances of damage to your PC by power surge and thermal shock by not switching it on and off any more than is necessary. Leave it on if you use it throughout the day and use Power Management in Control Panel to minimise power consumption if it's going to be idle for long periods. Fitting a surge protector to the mains lead, and unplugging the telephone lead during thunderstorms is a good idea, and not messing around with the insides of your PC – unless you know what you are doing – is highly recommended! If your PC operates in a smoky or dusty environment you should regularly give your disk drives a run-through with good quality floppy and CD-ROM cleaners, otherwise a clean up every two or three months should be sufficient.

BACKUP AND SURVIVE

Consider the worst case scenario. Your PC has crashed and all attempts – including those we've already outlined – have failed to revive it. Windows and all data on the hard disk has been corrupted and the only solution is to wipe the hard disk drive and start again by re-installing Windows and all of your applications. If that ever happened to you, how much work would you lose and how long would it take to get your PC back to the condition it was in before the crash?

If you've backed up your essential data a fatal crash need be nothing more than an inconvenience. Essentially there are two basic backup and recovery strategies: you can duplicate the entire contents of a hard disk, or just make copies of your data and system files. In both cases it's important to make backups at frequent intervals to keep the files up to date, though this can be scheduled to take place automatically and to save time it can be done incrementally, so that only the changes to the original backup are recorded. Backups or copies of backups should be stored in safe place, preferably 'off-site' so that in the event of a fire or similar catastrophe your backups will survive. Backup systems and data should also be tested from time to time; to make sure they actually work!

The 'whole disk' method sounds easy but in practice it's not that simple. To begin with you will need a reliable disk or tape-based recording system with sufficient capacity to store possibly several tens of gigabytes of data. Making the initial backup could take a very long time, though it would be a one-off job and subsequent updates will be much quicker. Reinstalling an entire system to a freshly formatted disk can be a real headache since without Windows or the original backup program on the drive there's no easy way of transferring the data from the disk or tape. More importantly, the backup may contain the source of the original crash – a bug or a virus – which could be unleashed to wreak havoc all over again. At the very least you'll be reinstating all of the redundant files and clutter that was probably slowing down your previous installation.

Method two takes quite a bit longer to get your PC back up on its feet again. This will depend on the number of programs and the amount of data there is to restore, but on the plus side the PC gets a fresh start and you won't necessarily need to buy any new hardware or software. Windows 95 and 98 come with a utility called Backup for archiving important files to floppy disk or a suitable tape or disk-based recording system. (Incidentally, Backup doesn't work with some CD-ROM writers.) In Windows 95 and 98 Backup can be found in My Computer. Right-click on the C: drive icon, choose Properties and select the Tools tab. The only limitation is that Windows has to be on the hard disk to run the program so it can't be used to restore a system to a freshly formatted hard disk. Backup is not installed by default in Windows ME, though it can be installed from the CD-ROM and it can be found in the Add-ons folder.

There is plenty of good backup software on the market including an excellent little (550 kilobytes) shareware program called WinRescue that's well worth trying. It combines an advanced backup and compression utility with a very capable set of crash recovery tools that might even save you from having to format your disk in the first place! A 30-day trial version is available for download from www.tucows.com and other fine shareware libraries. Versions for Windows 95, 98 and ME are all available.

The big question is what should you backup? It is vitally important to have up to date copies of your PC's critical system files and the Windows Registry.

Windows 95 users can make an Emergency Recovery Disk or ERD; this saves critical system files, including Autoexec.bat, config.sys, command. com, win.ini and system.ini to a floppy disk. In the event of a crash they can be restored by running a program on the disk called erd.exe. The ERU program is on the Windows 95 CD-ROM. Use Windows Explorer to open the 'Other' folder then Misc and ERU. Double click the eru.exe icon to start the program and copy the files to a blank floppy.

System files in Windows 98 can be backed up by going to Start > Programs > Accessories > System Tools > System Information, click on the Tools menu, select System Configuration Utility, display the General tab and click the Create Backup button. The files are stored on the hard disk and can be recovered from the same window using the Restore Button window, assuming that Windows is running of course. . .

Windows ME has a highly competent system file backup utility called System Restore. It takes 'snapshots' of the PC's critical files automatically at preset intervals, allowing the machine to be returned to a previous configuration with a minimum of fuss. The only catch is that Windows has to be running, though it will run from Safe Mode.

Microsoft Backup in Windows 98, one way to protect vital
system and data files

The most important data files to backup are the ones that cannot be
replaced, in other words anything that was written or created on your PC.
That includes word processor and spreadsheet files but that's only the
beginning. If you have Internet and email account keep an archive of all of
your sent and received messages. Don't forget your address book and list of
favourite websites. Recent versions of Outlook Express hide downloaded
messages in an obscure location like: C:\WINDOWS\Application
Data\Identities\{128E08E0-20FD-11D4-B189-FA89D946EF6A}
\Microsoft\Outlook Express. Address book data can usually be found at:
C:\WINDOWS\Application Data\Microsoft\Address Book. The Internet
Explorer Favourites file can also be found in the Windows folder, or you can
export it to a floppy disk by right clicking on Favourites on the Start menu.

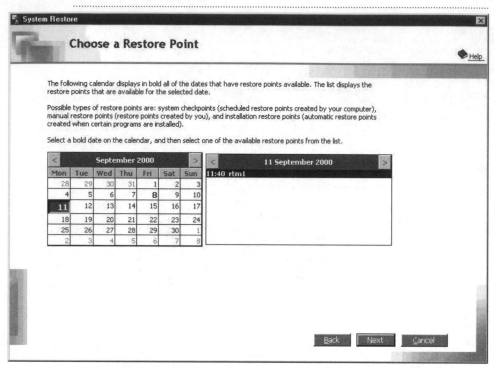

Windows ME has an excellent backup and restore facility

If you have any graphics programs and imaging devices, such as a scanner or digital camera, make sure you backup all of your image files (including any custom backgrounds, wallpaper or desktop themes). If there are a lot of them it's a good idea to use a file compression utility such as WinZip or PKZip, also available from shareware libraries on the Internet. Gather together any useful programs you have downloaded from the Internet and put the executable programs and 'zips' together in a folder so they can be saved en-masse. Finally, take a 'snapshot' of your desktop or any other part of your system that you want to restore. Just press the Print Screen button on the keyboard, open Paint or your chosen graphics program, paste the image, give the file a name and include it with the rest of your backups. Finally, cross your fingers and touch wood that you'll never need to use your backups.

Q&A   **Real world problems**

Spare stack pages

Q   My computer displayed the following message just before the desktop screen appeared: 'There are no spare stack pages. It may be necessary to increase the setting of 'MinSPs' in system.ini to prevent possible stack faults. There are currently 3 SPs allocated'. What on earth are stack pages and what if anything should I do about this message? It has not appeared on subsequent occasions that I have switched on.
C.W. via e-mail

A   Stack pages are 4-kilobyte chunks of memory that Windows automatically sets aside for emergencies, to prevent the system from crashing if it unexpectedly runs out of memory space when loading device drivers. By default Windows allocates 2 spare stack pages, most of the time two is enough but occasionally – often for no apparent reason – it proves insufficient. The solution is to increase the number of spare stack pages. Open system.ini with Notepad (Start > Programs > Accessories) click on Open on the File menu (change Files of type to All Files) and look for system.ini in the Windows folder. Scroll down the list to find the section heading [386Enh], it should be fairly close to the top, at the end of that section add the following line: 'MinSPs=4' (without the inverted commas and there are no spaces), save the file and restart your PC. If it happens again try increasing the number of spare stack pages further but it must be in multiples of 4.

Invalid VxD

Q   I get an error message from time to time, it says 'Invalid VxD dynamic link call from NWREDIR(04) + 000000D0 to device "0487", service 6'. I would love to have this explained in proper English.
K.W. via e-mail

A   Proper English is a bit of a tall order, but here goes. Invalid Dynamic Link Call error messages are usually caused by damaged, missing or incompatible drivers – data files that tell programs and peripherals how to interact with Windows. It's always worth uninstalling and re-installing the last program or device, before the problem started. The actual message is divided into three parts that can be expressed as follows: Invalid VxD dynamic link call from (Part 1) to device (Part 2) to service (Part 3). Part 1 is the driver's name or identity, part 2 is the name of the device or program it is associated with, in your case 0487 refers to 'NWLINK' which is the IPX/SPX-compatible Network Protocol. Part 3 is a fault code that tells the programmer which part of the program was requested, but could not be found.

Your error code suggests that the problem lies with Windows Dial Up Networking, so try removing and re-installing the Communications components on the Windows tab in Add/Remove programs in Control Panel. There are several books on the subject of error messages but they're mostly written by experts, for experts. It's always worth typing an error message in to an Internet search engine's Find field, and see what that throws up.

Building DMI data

Q   I am experiencing a problem when my computer boots up. During the initial start-up procedure and the black DOS screens I sometimes get a message at the bottom saying 'Building DMI Data'. The computer then stops at this screen. The only cure seems to be to turn the computer off and back on again. Sometimes the error recurs but after a few attempts it goes through the full start-up sequence and functions correctly. When it works properly the message reads 'Verifying DMI Data Pool'. What is DMI Data, and how do I remedy the problem?
R.R. via e-mail

A   This is a common error message and it often happens when the disk drive has been partitioned, formatted or replaced. DMI or the Desktop Management Interface is a set of instructions and a database of information (the 'Pool') used to setup and manage the PC during boot up. Often it can be resolved from the PC's BIOS (basic input output system) setup program. There are various methods, including restoring the default settings, to disconnecting or disabling the disk drive and forcing the PC to reconfigure itself. There is a very a helpful technical bulletin on disk drive manufacturer Maxtor's website at:

http://www.maxtor.com/technology/infobulls/15007.html

Device file missing

Q   Every time I boot up, the process stalls with a message telling me that 'A device file that may be needed to run Windows or a Windows application' is missing. 'If you deleted the file on purpose, try uninstalling the associated application using its uninstall or setup program. If you still want to use the application … try reinstalling … to replace the missing file. C:\ WINDOWS\SYSTEM\VMM32\vflat.vxd. Press a key to continue.' Can you please suggest what this file is and where I might start looking for it? *K.R. via e-mail*

A   It's a long and complicated story, and a fairly common complaint that affects a lot of Windows PCs causing shutdown problems, crashes and mouse misbehaviour. Suffice it to say you can replace the file from your Windows CD, and several others that your system may be missing, using a simple utility called vxdfix, obtainable from the following site:

http://users.megapath.net/~revolution/vxdfix.html

For a fuller (though not necessarily very clear) explanation of the problem have a look at the site's FAQ.

Cannot find specified file

Q   Every time I start Windows 98 I get the following warning: 'Unable to load Dynamic Link Library msnp32.dll. System cannot find the file specified.' How can I get rid of this annoying alarm that I have to acknowledge to enable boot up to be completed. *N.H. via e-mail*

A   This error message often follows an abortive attempt to install Internet access software, a new browser or changes to the settings in Dial Up Networking (DUN). During the installation file names are added to the Windows Registry but for one reason or another they are not copied to the hard disk. When Windows loads it looks for the files but cannot find them. Removing and then reinstalling Dial Up Networking can often cure it but before you do, make a note of all the settings. To do that double click on the DUN icon on My Computer, right click on your ISP connection icon, select Properties and note down the phone numbers and settings on each of the tabbed windows. To remove DUN go to Add/Remove Programs in Control Panel and the Windows setup tab. Double Click Communications and uncheck the box next to Dial Up Networking, select Close then OK and restart the PC. Go back to Add/Remove Programs in Control Panel, Windows setup and Communications and this time put a check in the DUN box, close and restart. Hopefully the error message will be no more. Finish off by making sure that your original Dial Up Networking settings have been correctly restored.

Fatal error UI skins

Q My computer, which is less than a year old, has developed a strange habit. When I first turn it on a message appears saying 'Fatal Error – Problems using the UI skins'. Please can you tell me if it really is fatal and what I can do to get rid of it? It really is a bit scary.
M.M. via e-mail

A Fortunately it's not as bad as it sounds. It's caused by corrupted or missing files associated with the Macromedia Shockwave player, a graphics utility for displaying interactive web content, included with most versions of Windows and Internet browsers. The solution is to reinstall Shockwave; try downloading the latest version from the Macromedia website at:

http://www.macromedia.com/software/

CMOS checksum

Q My PC at home now displays the message 'CMOS checksum error – load defaults?' when booting up after being switched off for more than 2–3 hours. Give us a clue!
J.C. via e-mail

A The backup battery that powers your PC's internal clock has expired; they generally last between 3 and 5 years. If you know your way around the inside of a PC you may be able to replace it yourself; if in doubt ask an expert.

Spool 32

Q Now and again a warning banner is displayed on start-up, which states that Spool 32 has performed an illegal operation and will be closed down. 'OK' removes this and nothing else seems to be wrong, all then works smoothly. What is Spool 32? Can it be removed altogether? If so, how?
R.W. via e-mail

A Spool 32 is a program within Windows that speeds up multiple printing jobs by temporarily storing each one on the hard disk drive, before being sent to the printer. The Spool 32 error message is very common and there are dozens of possible causes but most of them come down to other programs interfering with the print process, a corrupt printer driver or your PC is very low on resources (less than 100Mb free space, etc.). Try reinstalling your printer software and have a look at your printer manufacturer's website to see if there's an updated driver for your model or anything about error messages in the support or FAQ sections. Before printing exit all other programs that use the printer, in particular any fax software you may have. If all else fails and your printer is not very heavily used you can safely disable print spooling, without any significant reduction in performance. Go to Start > Settings > Printers, right click on your printer and select Properties, select the Details tab, click the Spool Settings button and check the item 'Print Directly to the Printer'.

MMSYSTEM.DLL Rundll

Q When I switch on my computer a sign comes up which says 'Rundll has caused an error in MMSYSTEM.DLL Rundll will now close. If you continue to experience problems try restarting your computer'. No matter how many times I restart my computer it still occurs. Is there any way I can correct this?
J.F. via e-mail

A This is quite a common error message, usually caused by a corrupt or missing command in an important start-up file called System.ini; you'll find the remedy in a Microsoft Knowledgebase article at:

http://support.microsoft.com/support/kb/articles/q138/8/35.asp

Those **** bleeps ...

Q   For some time now I have been trying to get rid of some irritating beeps heard as Windows 98 is starting up. I have the sound turned down everywhere I can find, but to no avail.
A.S. via e-mail

A   Those bleeps are there to help you. They are part of the Power On Self-Test (POST) routine conducted by the PC's BIOS (Basic Input Output System) program that checks the hardware on your machine, prior to loading Windows. If you hear more than one bleep there's usually something wrong! You can't turn the beeps off because they're heard through the PC's internal speaker (unless you disconnect it, but that would be inadvisable). There's a good explanation of what they mean, covering most popular makes of BIOS at:

   http://www.pchell.com/hardware/beepcodes.shtml

CHAPTER 6 **The BIOS and Registry**

*Between them the BIOS and the Windows Registry
are almost entirely responsible for how a PC
behaves, or misbehaves, so they are well worth
getting to know ...*

BIOLOGY OF THE BIOS

The Basic Input Output System or 'BIOS' may not sound particularly
interesting but it is arguably the single most important piece of software on
your PC. The BIOS's job is to initialise and configure a collection of inert
electronic and electromechanical components and turn them into a working
computer, ready to load and use the operating system, which for most of us
is Windows.

The BIOS program resides in a read-only memory or ROM microchip
on the PC's motherboard. It is stored in a chip because when it is powered up
your PC's processor or CPU has no idea what devices are attached to the
system, let alone how to use them, so it would be pointless storing such a
program on the hard disk drive. This also means the computer can still 'boot
up', even if the disk drive is faulty, or absent.

On early PCs the BIOS program was a fixed entity and the only way to
alter it was to replace the ROM chip or the entire motherboard. Nowadays
most BIOS programs are held in an erasable programmable read only
memory or EPROM chip, which means it is possible to update or change
the information, to accommodate new developments in hardware and
software. However this is a mixed blessing since virus programs have been
created that can infiltrate or corrupt the BIOS, turning a PC into a useless
pile of junk. More importantly even minor changes to the BIOS program
can have major consequences to your PC's good nature so we'll start off
with a general warning to look but don't touch, and never fiddle with the
BIOS on your PC unless you know exactly what you are doing.

Settings and adjustments for the BIOS are held in a separate memory chip called a CMOS (complimentary metal oxide silicon) which, unlike the ROM or EPROM chips used to store the BIOS program is 'volatile'. In other words it has to be permanently powered. This is done with a backup battery, which also maintains the PC's internal clock. Backup batteries generally last around five years; the first sign that it is failing is usually erratic timekeeping, but if after switch-on you see an error message 'CMOS checksum invalid' or 'Invalid configuration, run Setup', then that is a sure sign that the battery needs replacing.

One of the BIOS program's most important jobs is to carry out a series of diagnostic checks on the main motherboard components, including the RAM memory chips and input/output devices; this is called the Power On Self-Test or POST and it happens a few seconds after you've switched on. Normally the POST goes smoothly; on many PCs you'll hear a single short bleep from the internal speaker confirming that all's well, and Windows will begin loading. However, if you hear more than one bleep, a continuous tone or a repeated sequence of bleeps, that is a sure sign of trouble.

The number and pattern of bleeps or error code indicates the nature of the fault but this varies significantly according to the make and type of BIOS. You can find out more by first noting the name and version of your PC's BIOS – it appears on the monitor screen for a few moments after switch-on – and then consulting the appropriate manufacturer's website, or by visiting:

http://sysopt.earthweb.com/biosbmc.html or
http://www.pchell.com/hardware/beepcodes.shtml

These sites list the most common types of error code by manufacturer. Most faults are well beyond the scope of the average PC user but occasionally an error code points to an unseated memory module or adaptor card or a loose connecting cable, which the more intrepid amongst you can attempt to remedy.

POST error messages often appear following a major upgrade, replacing a hard drive, adding extra memory or changing the CPU. Since there are so many possibilities we can only generalise but more often than not the solution is to update the PC's BIOS. You may be lucky and find a reference to the problem in the new hardware's manual or troubleshooting guide; if not check the company's website, and the BIOS manufacturer's website for details of any known problems and solutions.

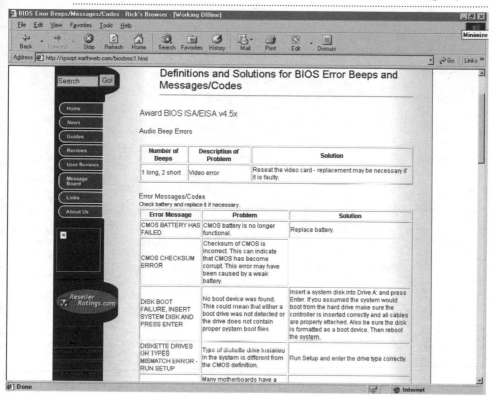

Websites such as this one can help you to decode BIOS bleep codes

At some point you may need to access your PC's BIOS program, but you are strongly advised not to touch anything unless you know what you are doing. The precise method varies but on most BIOS's a message appears on the screen at switch on, saying something like 'Press DEL to enter SETUP', or a combination of keys. Do so and you will see the BIOS main menu. Your mouse probably won't be working so selections have to be made using the keyboard arrow up/down keys; to look at a particular menu highlight the entry and press Return. Once an item is selected changes are usually made with the Page Up/down keys, and confirmed with the Return key. To return to the main menu press the Esc key and quit the BIOS by selecting the item 'Exit without saving changes' or words to that effect. You may be prompted to confirm your decision; i.e. 'Are you sure?' in which case enter 'Y' for yes, and press Return. The PC should now continue to load Windows as normal.

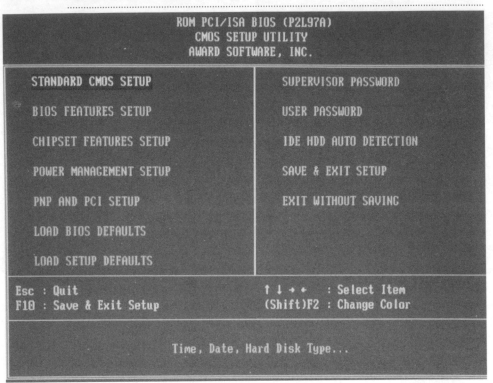

The opening menu of an Award BIOS program

Whilst your PC is working normally it is a good idea to make a record of your BIOS settings; you can do this easily if you have a printer connected to your PC, though be aware that some recent types of 'Windows only' printers may not work. Boot up your PC to the 'Setup' menu and switch on your printer. The items we're interested in are variously labelled 'Standard CMOS setup', 'Advanced CMOS Setup', 'BIOS Features', 'Chipset Features', 'Peripherals Setup', 'Integrated Peripherals' and 'Power Management'. The precise wording may be different and you can ignore anything to do with passwords, auto configuration and saving or exiting setup at this stage.

Select each item in turn with the arrow up/down keys and press Return, and when the menu appears press the Print Screen key. All being well your printer will leap into action and print the contents of each page. If for any reason you can't get a printout, copy the information by hand, take a photograph, video the screens with a camcorder, or use a BIOS 'viewer' utility like System Analyser. A trial version can be downloaded from:

http://www.tweakfiles.net/diagnostic/systemanalyser.html

If you get into trouble and haven't got a record of your PC's BIOS you can usually restore some sort of order by using the default settings or auto-configuration utility on the menu (i.e. 'Load Setup Defaults' or 'Auto Configuration with Fail-Safe Settings', etc). One last piece of advice, if you do feel inspired to make alterations only change one thing at a time. Exit the BIOS after saving each change and boot to Windows, to make sure that everything is still working properly.

CLOSE UP

The precise contents of BIOS programs vary but it's worth looking at some of the most common features. Our first port of call is the Standard CMOS Setup menu, which is usually the first item on the menu. This contains the adjustment for the PC's internal clock and calendar: you can change it if necessary using the keyboard's arrow and page up/down keys. Note that this is not the same as the Windows Time and Date settings, which gets its information from the CMOS clock, so if that's wrong, the Windows clock will be wrong as well. You should also see information about your PC's disk drives, though these days most BIOS's use automatic settings so there may not be much actual data on display. This page should report on your PC's RAM memory and there may be an option to change the colour of the BIOS menus (usually by pressing F2 on Award and Ami BIOS's). When you've finished press the Esc key to return to the main menu and select the next item, which is normally Advanced CMOS or BIOS Features Setup.

It probably looks a bit intimidating but don't worry, most of it is to do with motherboard configuration and only concerns manufacturers and those building their own PCs. On some BIOS's you get a short explanation of what each item does when it's highlighted, or there may be a Help facility (usually F1) but if you want to know more there are plenty of books on the subject, including the seminal work, *The BIOS Companion* by Phil Croucher (ISBN: 0968192807).

Most of the settings you should leave well alone; in any case they are likely to be the factory defaults, unless your PC was specially built or configured, but one item you might feel like changing is 'Boot up Num Lock', which decides whether or not the keyboard's numeric pad is enabled

```
                 AMIBIOS SETUP - STANDARD CMOS SETUP
           (C)1996 American Megatrends, Inc. All Rights Reserved

Date (mm/dd/yyyy): Wed  Jul  12,2000          Base Memory: 640 KB
Time (hh/mm/ss)  : 21:04:23                   Extd Memory: 31 MB

Floppy Drive A:     1.44 MB 3½

                                              LBA  Blk  PIO  32Bit
             Type         Size Cyln Head WPcom Sec Mode Mode Mode Mode
Pri Master : Auto                                 On   On   Auto On
Pri Slave  : CDROM                                On   On   Auto On



Boot Sector Virus Protection     Disabled

Month:  Jan - Dec                             ESC:Exit  ↑↓:Sel
  Day:  01 - 31                               PgUp/PgDn:Modify
 Year: 1901 - 2099                            F2/F3:Color
```

The Standard CMOS setup screen, most used for time and date
settings and basic hard drive parameters

at switch on. Another one is Boot Up Sequence. This determines the order
of the disk drives your PC accesses to look for system files when it boots up.
The default is usually A:, C:, CD-ROM but if you change it to C:, A: etc.,
boot up may be a little quicker, and you can leave a floppy disk in the drive.
Just remember to change back to A:, C:, if the PC ever fails to boot, so you
can use your emergency start-up disk.

Tucked away on the list you may see a Password or Security option. By
default it's usually set to 'Setup' which means you can password protect the
BIOS menu, but if you change it to 'System' this will stop the boot up
process until the correct password is entered. To create a password, go back
to the main menu and select the User Password option (if you also set up the
Supervisor Password you'll protect the BIOS as well). This offers a high
degree of protection because it prevents Windows from loading so there's
no easy way to 'hack' into the machine, just make sure you remember your
password!

Next is the Peripherals Setup or Integrated Peripherals Setup menu: look for 'Printer Port' or 'LPT1'. Most BIOS's default to a 'standard' or 'normal' setting for data transfer through the printer port, which is safe but slow and can cause problems with some recent peripherals that share the printer port. Changing the setting to ECP or EPP (or ECP + EPP on some BIOS's) may solve current or future compatibility problems and yield a small improvement in printer performance; it's certainly worth trying. You should be warned of any conflicts when you exit the BIOS and boot to Windows.

Our final stop is the Power Management menu. This is an important one with settings that decide how your PC behaves when it's not being used. It's usually a good idea to play safe and use Windows Advanced Power Management (Start > Settings > Control Panel); the BIOS options are very detailed and really only for experts. Nevertheless there may be one or two things you might want to have a look at. Power Switch or Power Button

```
         AMIBIOS SETUP - PERIPHERAL SETUP
     (C)1996 American Megatrends, Inc. All Rights Reserved

Com1 Port                   3F8h        Available Options:
Com2 Port(IR)               2F0h          Normal
   IR Mode                  IrDA          Bi-Dir
      IR DMA Channel        1             EPP
LPT Port                    378           ECP
   LPT Extended Mode        EPP
   EPP Version              1.9
   LPT Port DMA Channel     N/A
Audio Device                Enable
   Audio I/O                220h
   Audio IRQ Channel        IRQ 5
   Audio DMA Channel 1      DMA #0
   Audio DMA Channel 2      DMA #3
   FM Synthesizer           Enabled
   MIDI Port                300h
   WSS Port                 530h
Port Replicator Joystick    Disabled

                                        ESC:Exit  ↑↓:Sel
                                        PgUp/PgDn:Modify
                                        F2/F3:Color
```

The Peripherals Setup menu; it's a good idea to check your printer port settings changes how the PC's on/off switch works (Instant Off, Off After 4 Seconds, etc., manual off, etc.) and there may be an option to disable the facility that switches the PC on when the phone rings (Power on Modem Action), which some users find incredibly annoying.

If you make any changes to the BIOS, save and exit as normal and be on the look out for any unexpected error messages as it boots up.

THE WINDOWS REGISTRY

The Windows Registry is a huge database containing critical settings that determine how Windows and all of the software and hardware used by your PC works, which is why Microsoft has gone to the trouble of hiding it well away from novice users – you have been warned!

Changes to the Registry are carried out when you install new software or hardware, or if you alter desktop settings via the Control Panel or with utilities like Tweak UI. Under normal circumstances there is no reason why you should need to go anywhere near the actual files; however the Registry is often directly involved in crashes or malfunctions and a little background knowledge might prove useful if your PC starts misbehaving; if nothing else an insight into the workings of your PC is empowering and can help dispel some of the mystery.

Registry data is contained in two files called 'user.dat' and 'system.dat' and they are stored in the main Windows folder. Because of their importance they are automatically backed up. Windows 95 makes copies every time it boots up successfully, called 'system.dao' and 'user.dao'. Windows 98 and ME are even more cautious and keeps up to five recent copies of the Registry and critical system files (system.ini & win.ini) in a Windows folder called Sysbckup (they're usually called rb00.cab, etc.). As a further precaution all versions of Windows also keep a copy of the Registry when it was first installed on your PC, this is called 'system.1st' and lives in the root directory of the C: drive. An expert can use this file to get your PC working when all other attempts to restore the Registry have failed. More routine problems with a 'corrupt' Registry – caused by faulty software or a failed installation – may generate an error message to the effect that Windows will revert to a saved backup, if you are given the option it is wise to click OK and let your PC carry out the procedure.

Before we go any further it's a good idea to know how to make a manual backup of your PC's Registry so you can easily restore it should something go amiss. You should do it before you make any changes to the Registry, in fact get into the habit of doing it every time you open Regedit. Start by deciding where to keep your backup file; it should be somewhere you can easily find it or better still, create a special folder for the purpose. Open Windows Explorer, click once on the Drive C: icon to highlight it then go to the File menu. Select New click on Folder and an icon called 'New Folder' appears at the bottom of the screen. The name should be highlighted, press backspace to clear the text field and rename the folder Myback, or something equally memorable, press Return then close or minimise Explorer and return to Regedit. Go to the Registry drop-down menu and select Export Registry File. In 'Save In' navigate your way to your newly created Myback folder and in the 'File Name' field call it something like Regbak, click Save and it's done. This will create a text file called regbak.reg, if you ever need to restore the Registry after an editing session

Regedit, the Windows Registry editor utility, the first step is to make a backup simply double-click on Regbak.reg, you will be asked if you want to 'add the information to the Registry . . .', click yes and the file will be restored.

You can view the Registry, and make manual changes to the data (though don't be tempted just yet!) with a hidden Windows utility called Regedit. On the Start menu select Run and type 'regedit' (without the inverted commas of course) and an Explorer type window opens. To close Regedit simply click on the 'X' in the top right hand corner or select Exit on the Registry menu.

For the sake of clarity Registry data files are presented as single directory tree with six 'branches' in the left-hand pane. At the top is HKEY_CLASSES_ROOT; this contains details about which files are associated with which programs, shortcut data and information about Object Linking and Embedding or OLE. This is the way Windows allows bits of information (text, graphics, images, etc.) to be copied between and inserted into different applications.

The second branch is HKEY_CURRENT_USER and this includes the personal preferences (appearance, colour schemes, screen saver, etc.) of whoever is logged onto the PC at the time. HKEY_LOCAL_MACHINE stores general settings and preferences for all of the PC's hardware and software. HKEY_USERS is where the details of everyone who is logged onto the machine are kept. HKEY_CURRENT_CONFIG contains more information about the way the PC is set up, and lastly HKEY_DYN_DATA, which is a record of all of Windows Plug and Play features that changes as and when devices are added or removed from the system.

Each branch of the tree is known as a Hive, containing folders called Keys and Sub Keys, which hold the 'Values', the actual data that makes the Registry tick. Values are stored in the form of alphanumeric text and binary or hexadecimal code.

One way of getting better acquainted with the Registry is to try a few simple tweaks but do bear in mind earlier warnings about always making a backup first. In fact we're not going to attempt anything too challenging or hazardous, just a few quick and simple adjustments that add some extra functionality and change the way several Windows 95 and 98 (but not ME) features look and work. It's all very straightforward but be aware that Regedit will not warn you if you make a mistake, or prompt you to confirm actions when you close the registry editor! We'll kick off with a nice easy one, changing the name of the Recycle Bin on the desktop, which a lot of people detest.

Open Regedit and make the all-essential backup then work your way down through the following set of keys: HKEY_LOCAL_MACHINE/ SOFTWARE/CLASSES/CLSID/ {645FF040-5081-101B-9F08-00AA002F954E} (be warned that CLSID and that long string of numbers and letters are a long way down the list). Click on the entry and an item called Default appears in the right-hand pane, with the name 'Recycle Bin' in the Data column. Double click on the icon next to Default and the Edit String dialogue box appears with the words Recycle Bin highlighted in the Value Data field. Press backspace to delete it and type in your new name. Click OK, move the mouse pointer to an empty area of the desktop, click the left mouse button once then press F5 to refresh the desktop and the name will change.

Here's how to get rid of a Windows annoyance, the names of programs left behind in the Add/Remove Programs list, after the program has been deleted. (Actually you can also do this with Tweak UI, but this method is much more fun . . .) Go to: HKEY_LOCAL_MACHINE\Software\ Microsoft\Windows\CurrentVersion\Uninstall and the full list of titles in Add/Remove Programs appears. To remove the name key of a program you've already deleted simply right-click on it and select Delete.

This one is for Windows 98 users who have upgraded from Windows 95 and miss the way the Start menu used to open with side-by-side columns, instead of the single scrolling list in Win 98. In Regedit navigate through the following list of keys: HKEY_LOCAL_MACHINE\Software\ Microsoft\Windows\CurrentVersion\explorer\Advanced place the mouse pointer in the right-hand pane and right-click, New appears and on the drop-down menu choose String Value, rename it to 'StartMenuScroll Programs', double click the new icon and in the Value Data field type 'false', close Regedit and give it a try.

Control Panel is the probably the most frequently used Windows Utilities, yet it is buried away on the Settings menu or has to be accessed from My Computer. This next Registry hack puts the contents of Control Panel in a sub folder on the Start Menu, so you can get at anything with just one mouse click. This time there's no need to actually go into the Registry to make the changes, instead right-click on the Start button and select Open. When the Explorer Windows opens go to New on the File menu and select Folder and a new folder icon appears, backspace to clear the name and type in the following: 'Control Panel.{21EC2020-3AEA-1069-A2DD-08002B30309D}', do not forget the dot after Control Panel, press Return and the folder's name should now change to Control Panel. Close the Start

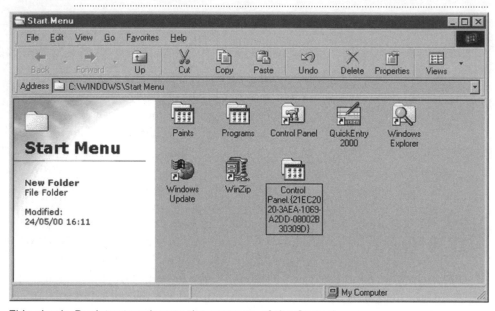

This simple Registry tweak puts the contents of the Control Panel on your Start menu

Menu window and a new item called Control Panel appears on the Start Menu that opens to show its contents.

The brown desktop Briefcase icon is a bit dull, so why not change it for a smart metal one? Open Regedit and drill down through the keys thus: HKEY_CLASSES_ROOT\CLSID\{85BBD920-42A0-1069-AE24-08002B30309D}\DefaultIcon. In the right-hand pane you should see a Default icon, next to it in the Data column it should read 'c:\windows\System\syncui.dll,0, if so click on the icon to open the Edit String dialogue box and change the 0 at the end to a 1, click OK and close Regedit, click onto the desktop and press the F5 key to refresh the display and hey–presto, a shiny new aluminium case. (On some machines you may have to re-boot Windows for the change to take effect.)

The name of the Registered Owner of your PC, which appears on the front page of System Properties (right-click My Computer and select Properties) is often set by the vendor or manufacturer. You can easily change it to your name by editing the Registry. Click on the plus sign next to HKEY_LOCAL_MACHINE and then on the plus signs next to the following Keys: Software/Microsoft/Windows and double-click on CurrentVersion. Scroll down the list of items that appears in the right-hand pane until you come to 'RegisteredOwner', double-click on the icon next to it and the Edit String dialogue box opens, with the name that was entered when Windows was first installed. Press backspace to delete the entry and type in a new name, click OK and exit Regedit.

That is just a very brief taste of what the Registry can do. If you want to go any further you should read up on the subject; there are plenty of detailed books, including the inevitable 'Dummies' Guides and there's a huge amount of information on the Internet, along with very many more hacks. A very good place to start is:

http://home.aol.com/AXCEL216/reg.htm

Q&A **Real world problems**

Wake up call

Q Every now and again I find that the ringing of the phone switches on the computer. Is there any way of preventing this happening? If I switch off at the mains, which are not easily accessible, how long will it take for the clock to cease working? I feel that this is wearing out the computer as I have to switch it off and reboot after switching on the printer in order for the printer to work. *M.P. via e-mail*

A 'Wake up on ring' is one of your PC's power management functions, it's controlled by the BIOS. This is normally accessed by pressing the Delete key (or a combination of keys) during boot up, there's usually a message, something like, 'to enter set-up program press . . .'. When the BIOS menu appears look for the Power Management menu (follow the on-screen instructions to make selections). Be very careful not to make any accidental changes, you're looking for an entry like 'Power up on modem', and disable if necessary.

What's in a name?

Q A friend recently set up my computer after installing a new hard disk and he has entered my surname beginning with a lower case letter instead of an upper case one. As a proof-reader I find it very irritating and would like to know where I am able to change it to have a capital letter at the beginning of my surname.

S.C. via e-mail

A   A PC's registered owner name – entered during the installation of Windows – is stored in the Registry (the owner's name and 'organisation' is also used by other applications when they are installed). To change it open the Registry Editor by clicking Start, then Run and typing 'regedit' (without the quote marks) into the Open field, and click OK. Before you do anything else make a backup of the Registry by clicking on Export Registry File on the Registry drop-down menu. Call the file 'regbak' and save it in My Documents or somewhere you will remember to find it. This creates a self-installing file called regbak.reg; if anything goes wrong you can restore the Registry by double clicking on regbak.reg.

Back now to Regedit. In the left-hand window click on the plus signs next to the following entries: HKEY_LOCAL_MACHINE\ SOFTWARE\Microsoft\Windows and double-click on CurrentVersion. This opens up a set of files or 'keys' in the right-hand window, scroll down the list to find RegisteredOwner, right click on the entry and select modify (or double click), change the entry and click OK. You can also change the RegisteredOrganisation information in the same way. Exit Regedit and re-boot for the change to take effect.

Run stops

Q   The AutoRun facility on my Hitachi CDR-7730 CD-ROM does not work even though the 'Auto Insert Notification' in Device Properties is checked. Have you any other ideas?

O.P. via e-mail

A   It is possible that a Registry entry is causing the problem. Depending on your version of Windows the errant keys can be found at:

HKEY_LOCAL_MACHINE\SYSTEM\ControlSet001\Services\ CDRom

or

HKEY_LOCAL_MACHINE\SYSTEM\CurrentControlSet\Services\ CDRom

Change the binary value of 'Autorun' from 0 (disable) to 1 and reboot.

Do not delete!

Q While trying to clean up and make space on the PC I came across a very large file, apparently created by the system itself, called user.dat whose purpose I cannot understand. It appears to have registered every instruction and setting since the beginning of time. What is its purpose and is it possible or safe to delete it or reduce it in size?
D.D. via e-mail

A Touch it at your peril! User.dat is one of two critical files in Windows (the other is called System.dat) that make up the 'Registry', which controls every aspect of Windows and all of the software on your PC.

Memory stealer

Q A colleague's PC displays '8Mb shared memory' (64Mb in total) shortly after the power on self-test (POST) sequence. Please advise where the setting for this is located and the likely reasons for it.
M.N. via e-mail

A Some motherboards with built-in video adaptors steal a chunk of memory from the PC's RAM; it's a sneaky way for manufacturers to be able to claim that a PC has '8Mb' of video memory. The allocation is usually best left alone but if you know what you are doing and want try another setting you'll have to access the PC's BIOS. Look in the Advanced Setup section, where you should see an item labelled 'Shared Memory Size'. Changing the allocation probably won't make any difference on text-based office type applications but it could cause problems on graphics-intensive software and games.

CHAPTER 7 **Reinstalling Windows**

There's a good argument for periodically wiping or 'formatting' a PC's hard disk and starting afresh every year or so. It's one way of avoiding the inevitable build up of file clutter, glitches and the gradual slow down that occurs on any well-used PC. For a few weeks or months afterwards it's like having a new machine all over again. The counter argument is that 'if it ain't broke, don't fix it'; removing and reinstalling Windows plus all of your applications and data files can be a long and tedious job.

GETTING STARTED

Unfortunately leaving well alone is only an option for as long as the PC behaves itself... Sooner or later most Windows users will experience a catastrophic crash or if they're really unlucky, a fatal virus infection where the only solution is to start over or, worst of all, a complete hard disk failure, necessitating a replacement disk drive.

Wiping a PC's hard disk drive to reinstall Windows or faulty applications is a fairly drastic procedure and should be considered only as a last resort. Needless to say you will lose all of the files and data stored on it so make sure you have explored all other possibilities first. If Windows has become corrupted you could try reinstalling it by running the set-up program from the CD-ROM. There's a slim chance it might overwrite the damaged files. It's always worth trying the Scandisk utility to repair faults in the disk filing system and a lot of Windows problems, particularly those involving drivers, can be tracked down by starting in Safe Mode (see Chapter 2).

If you upgraded from Windows 95 to 98 you will be asked to provide details of your previous setup during the installation, so before you start have the disk and its serial number to hand. Windows 95 users must also have the driver disk for their CD-ROM drive – more about that in a moment. That shouldn't be necessary if you are using Windows 98 or ME, but it's a good idea to have it handy, just in case. Finally, and most important of all, you must have an emergency start-up disk for your PC. (In case you've forgotten double click on the Add/Remove Programs icon in Control Panel, select the Start-up disk tab and follow the instructions.)

If you are installing a new hard drive then you have to go through an additional procedure called 'partitioning' before you can load Windows. This is quite different to the formatting process so don't get the two confused. It helps if you think of a hard disk drive as a filing cabinet; partitioning is akin to deciding how many drawers it will have, formatting decides how the files in the draws are organised.

Until fairly recently most hard disk drives had a single partition but in the mid 1990s the capacity of hard disk drives increased dramatically and most versions of Windows were unable to handle drives larger than 2 gigabytes. To get around the limit larger disk drives had to be split up into 2-gigabyte (or less) partitions, which the operating system regarded as separate drives.

Later versions of Windows 95 and Windows 98 and ME use an improved data handling system called FAT 32, which allows disk drives with a capacity greater than 2Gb to be treated as a single drive. However, some PC makers and sellers still prefer to partition drives for the sake of convenience or for extra flexibility. In most cases Windows and all of the most frequently used programs will be in the C: partition whilst other partitions, assigned drive letters D:, E: etc, can contain a complete set of Windows installation files, so it can easily be restored, should something go wrong. Partitions are also used for archiving or keeping large files separate from the rest of the programs on the disk, minimising the chances of them becoming lost or corrupted through the action of a virus. Partitions can also be used for 'dual-booting' a PC, allowing the user to switch between operating systems. For example one partition might contain Windows 98 and its programs whilst another could be used for Windows NT or Linux and associated applications.

If you are starting afresh with a new hard disk drive, then before you can use it, it has to be partitioned, otherwise if you only want to erase the drive and start over you can skip the next couple of paragraphs and proceed directly to Formatting.

PARTITIONING

To partition a disk drive you need a program or utility called Fdisk. Fdisk is included on your PC's Start-up or Emergency Boot disk. If the new drive is larger than 2Gb make sure the version of Fdisk supports FAT 32 – i.e. the boot disk was created using Windows 98 or ME or the OSR2 version of Windows 95.

After the new drive has been installed and all of the connections checked, and double-checked the partitioning process can begin. Pop in the Start-up disk, switch the machine on, the BIOS program carries out its diagnostic routine on the motherboard, memory and disk drives and if all's well a few moments later the A: prompt appears on the screen. Type 'fdisk' (without the quotation marks of course) press return and follow the instructions. When asked you should ensure that Partition 1 is 'active' as this will enable the PC to boot up from the new disk drive. When the job is finished re-boot the PC, run fdisk again, select option 4 to display the partition information and check that there are no error messages, the capacity shown is correct and that everything is okay.

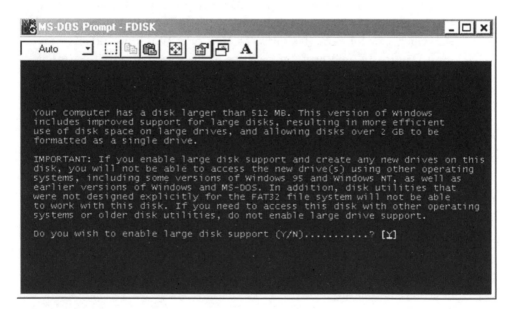

Before you reload Windows it's a good idea to wipe the slate
clean by partitioning the disk drive using the fdisk command

FORMATTING

Formatting a drive is quite straightforward, indeed you may already have done it before, when preparing a floppy disk for first use (though these days most floppies are sold 'pre-formatted'). Your PC must be in its default condition and ready to boot from a Start-up disk in drive A: when you are ready load your Boot disk and switch on, when the A: prompt appears type the following command: 'format c: /s' (without the quotation marks) and press the return key. The '/s' after format is important, it's a command 'switch' that instructs the PC to copy important system files onto the hard disk so that in future it can boot up on its own, without help from a floppy disk.

The length of time it takes to format a hard disk drive varies according to its capacity, so you may have to be patient. When it has finished remove the boot disk and restart the computer, this time the PC will boot up on its own and present you with a flashing C: prompt. If you get a message saying 'please insert boot disk' that means the vital system files haven't been copied from the floppy to the hard disk. In that case boot up from the floppy disk once more and when the A: prompt appears enter the command 'sys c:', and

Formatting your hard disk, an important step before installing Windows try again. If you experience recurrent problems during formatting – and that is quite unusual – it's worth starting over from the beginning and re-partitioning the drive in case vestiges of the old operating system or possibly even a virus has remained behind and is causing trouble. Occasionally there may be a physical problem with the drive, resulting in 'bad sectors' or parts of the drive that are unable to reliably store information, in which case there's nothing you can do but start again with a new drive.

LOADING WINDOWS

If everything has gone to plan at this point you now have a fully working but empty PC. The last job is to load the Windows operating system. If you are installing Windows from an 'upgrade' CD-ROM you will be asked to prove eligibility by temporarily loading a previous 'full' version of Windows, so have this to hand.

When loading or reloading Windows 98 or ME the system files that were copied to the hard drive during formatting should tell the PC to recognise the CD-ROM drive. The Windows 98 boot up disk contains a number of generic CD-ROM drivers covering most common makes and types of drive; however if your newly formatted PC doesn't recognise the CD-ROM drive you will have to use the installation disk that came with it. Pop in the disk, change to the A: drive and type 'dir'. This will show you what's on the disk, look for something called 'install.exe', 'setup' or 'cdinstall', type it in as it appears on the screen then press return and follow the instructions, it should only take a minute or two.

If the CD-ROM driver is installed, or you have successfully loaded it yourself, change to the drive letter for the CD-ROM drive, usually by typing D: (though it may be another letter if the drive is partitioned), type setup and the loading sequence will begin and you're well on the way to restoring your PC to its original condition.

Q&A   **Real world problems**

Exchange rate

Q   I'm about to change my PC and am worried about how I'm going to transfer valuable data from my old PC to the new one. I can cope with copying my Word templates and supplementary dictionary but don't know where my many Word 'AutoCorrect' entries live. How about all my personalised settings for Outlook Express? Must they all be re-input manually? These are just a couple of examples, there are many more when you think about it. Although transferring large amounts of data is tricky for those without zip drives, etc., in my (limited) experience much of this kind of data is usually held in small files easily put on a floppy.
T.L. via e-mail

A   The simplest method is to remove the hard disk drive from your old PC and temporarily install it in the new machine. You should change the 'jumpers' on the back to 'slave' mode – there should be a little diagram on the drive to show how it's done. Connect the drive to the spare plug on the ribbon cable going to the PC's drive (make sure it's the right way around) and a spare 3-pin power cable. When the PC boots up Windows will automatically recognise the old drive and assign it letter D: When you install programs like Word and Internet Explorer/Outlook Express they will scan all of the drives on your new machine, looking for previous versions and you will be asked if you want to use preferences and import data.

Occasionally it doesn't work, in which case, for Word copy the 'normal.dot' file from your old disk drive to the same location on the new drive, it can be found in: Windows/Application Data/Microsoft/Templates. Messages in Outlook Express 5 are filed in: Windows/Application Data/ Identities/(123 long number 456)/Microsoft/Outlook. You can use Windows Explorer to move any other data from the old drive, and when you've finished it can be removed, or used for additional storage. If you don't fancy installing the drive yourself ask the vendor of your new machine or a local PC dealer, who should be able to do it for you, for a modest fee. Alternatively you can set up a Direct Cable Connection between the two machines, effectively creating a simple network over which you can transfer files. Details of how to go about it are contained in Windows Help.

Pound notes

Q   After reloading Windows I have found that my keyboard cannot produce the pound sign. When holding down shift and pressing 3, I get # instead of £. Each time I want to use it, I have to use character map.
L.A.L. via e-mail

A   The most likely explanation is that the keyboard language setting in Windows was left on the US American default setting during installation. It can be changed to English (British) by clicking on the Keyboard icon in Control Panel (Start > Settings); select the Language tab, click the Add button scroll down the list to find the correct setting, highlight the entry and click OK.

Mute modem

Q   I am in the process of reinstalling everything onto a new hard disk. My problem is minor but irritating. Although I clearly heard my modem dialling up on my previous installation, it is now very faint. I have my modem volume control to maximum and all other sounds are okay. Any suggestions please, before it drives me mad?
A.M. via e-mail

A   One possibility is a disconnected or missing connecting lead, between the modem and your PC's soundcard. This may have been dislodged or not replaced when the new hard disk drive was installed. If the modem is an internal type look for an audio output socket on the back panel of your computer (it should be close to the telephone cable sockets). This should have a cable going to the audio input socket on the soundcard (next to the speaker or audio output socket). If the cable is present you could check volume and mute settings for the audio input. They can be found on the Volume Control, which is on the View Menu of the CD Player utility (Start > Programs > Accessories & Entertainment if you are using Windows 98).

Split decision

Q   I was running Windows 95 on my laptop with a 6 gigabyte hard disk drive partitioned across drives C, D & E; each of 2 gigabytes. I formatted my hard

drive and installed Windows 98 in place of 95. Everything went well and it works, perfectly; however, my hard disk remains resolutely split. How do I combine these three 'drives' into one C drive?
T.N. via e-mail

A   You cannot change disk partitions from within Windows but there are a number of utility programs on the market that can do the job, the best-known being Symantec Partition-IT Extra Strength and Power Quest's Partition Magic. However it's a bit of a palaver and unless the partitioning is causing you problems it's usually a good idea to leave well alone.

Save the faves

Q   I do weekly or fortnightly back-ups of essential data filed under My Documents on to my 250Mb Zip disk. I have an extensive list of favourite websites listed in Internet Explorer but don't know how to backup this list so that the settings can be restored in the event of total loss of data. Can this be done and if so how?
D.R. via e-mail

A   Include the Favourites folder in C:\Windows in your list of backups; if your original is lost or corrupted simply copy the contents of your backup into the Favourites folder.

ME mutterings

Q   I have just installed Windows ME after reading the review in Boot Camp review (dot.com September 21st) and it looks good. However, Windows Explorer has vanished from the Programs list and I can't find it anywhere.
M.J. via e-mail

A   Under the bonnet Windows ME and Windows 98 are very similar but there have been some changes in presentation, and a few compatibility problems are coming to light. Windows Explorer has moved to the Accessories list under Programs on the Start menu, but you can place a shortcut anywhere you like by holding down the Ctrl key, right-clicking on the Windows Explorer folder icon then dragging it to your preferred location.

ME incompatible?

Q Are you aware that Windows ME is incompatible with Norton AntiVirus 2000 and that there is no option to enter MS-DOS directly? I can't get full screen DOS – only a nasty little window.
Q.B. via e-mail

A Most programs and hardware devices seem to work perfectly well with Windows ME but there are exceptions and if problems occur your first stop should be the ME FAQ on the Microsoft website at:

http://support.microsoft.com/support/windows/topics/winme/software/softwarefaq.asp

There you will find an updated list of known problems, including the one with Norton AntiVirus 2000, which is apparently fairly easy to resolve.

You can still boot to MS-DOS, but not from Windows, the trick is to load the emergency recovery disk – that you're urged to make during installation – and when the Start-up menu appears, press F5.

CHAPTER 8 **Hands off! Securing Windows**

One of the things that surprises a lot of Windows users is the operating system's apparent lack of security features. Anyone with a mind to do so can easily interfere with key settings that can drastically affect the way a PC behaves, even stop it working altogether. Microsoft could have incorporated effective security measures as standard but good sense prevailed. Security systems have a nasty habit of backfiring and there is no doubt they would cause enormous problems, especially for inexperienced users – Windows without restrictions is bad enough. . .

SYSTEM POLICIES

In fact Windows 95 and 98 do come with a powerful security facility called the System Policy Editor or 'Poledit' but it is not installed by default, or readily accessible, unless you know what you are looking for. Microsoft in its wisdom has decided not to include Poledit in Windows ME, relying instead on the System Restore facility to repair damage done to PCs by the kind of unauthorised fiddling that Poledit is designed to prevent. Some elements of Poledit will work with ME but it is safer to assume that what follows is only applicable to Windows 95 and 98.

System Policy Editor is meant to be used by System Administrators. They're the folks who look after networks or a number of PCs, such as teachers and lecturers, who use it to stop mischievous students messing around with desktop settings and running illicit programs. Clearly it could also be of interest to anyone whose PC is shared by several people, particularly if they include meddlesome children.

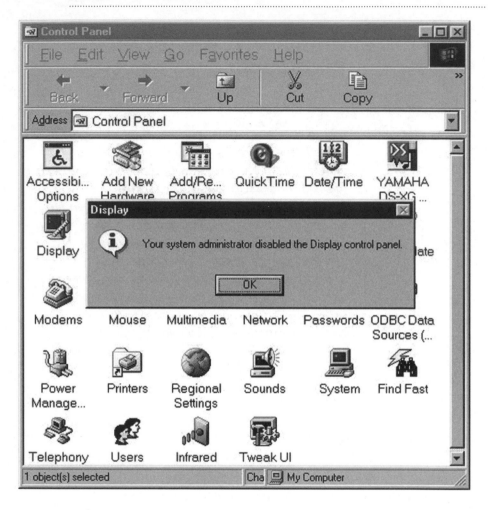

System Policies can stop people tinkering with your PC

Poledit is not especially difficult to use but it can easily muck up your computer, so leave it alone unless you are confident of your abilities and are prepared to accept the consequences, and don't blame us if you get it wrong!

Poledit covers a lot of ground but the part we're interested in is basically a tool for editing the Windows Registry (see Chapter 6). Poledit lives on the Windows 95 and 98 installation disks. Unlike most other Windows utilities Poledit is not loaded into the PC during setup nor is it accessible from Control Panel or the desktop. It is possible to install it on your PC's hard disk drive if you wish but that would defeat the object and compromise security. Ensuring that the installation disk has to be loaded every time in order to make changes is a useful first line of defence against casual tinkering by PC-savvy users (though obviously it can't stop determined fiddlers, who may have their own copy of Poledit on a floppy or CD-ROM. . .).

Windows 95 and 98 have different versions of Poledit. The Windows 95 one is slightly simpler in presentation and therefore easier for beginners to get to grips with, moreover it appears to work on Windows 98 PCs without any problems; however it's sensible to play safe and use the one that came with your version of Windows. The main difference is that Poledit in Windows 98 contains a number of extra features, mostly designed to control Internet and e-mail facilities. To keep things as simple as possible we'll stick to the basic features common to both versions. If you want to know more about what Poledit can do there are plenty of websites and books covering the subject.

The changes made by Poledit on a stand-alone PC are usually global and will affect everyone who uses that computer; however it's possible to confine the changes to single 'profiles', where the PC is used by a number of people with different passwords.

Before you do anything it's a good idea to work out exactly what you want to achieve since too many restrictions can be just as bad as none at all and you could end up making your PC difficult or impossible to use for routine tasks. To help you decide we'll round off this section with a run down of some of the available options.

Poledit controls how the PC works using a series of 'administration templates'. There are several of them, mostly dealing with advanced network operations. However, the one we're interested in concerns the Control Panel, the Desktop, access to the Windows filing system and disk drives. The Control Panel options include the facility to hide the Background, Appearance and Settings tabs on the Display icon. The latter allows users to change screen resolution, which can create a lot of problems. Incidentally, Smart Alecs who know how to get into Control Panel by various alternative methods (right-clicking on the desktop and selecting Properties, My Computer, Windows Explorer, etc.) will not be able to get around the restrictions, they will be greeted with a message advising them that 'Your System Administrator has disabled the Display Control Panel' and they won't be able to make any changes. Other Control Panel items that can be restricted or disabled include Networks, Printers, Passwords and

System, which includes the important Device Manager and Hardware Profiles tabs.

Poledit can lock Windows wallpaper and colour schemes and again will defeat any scurrilous attempts to make changes by backdoor means, such as using Internet Explorer to set new wallpaper. Poledit can also remove the Run Command from the Start menu, turn off Folder Options and Taskbar & Start Menu on Settings on the Start Menu. It can hide disk drives in My Computer, make everything vanish from the desktop, disable the Shut Down command and cancel the feature whereby desktop settings are automatically saved on exit. Finally to scupper any serious attempts at sabotage Poledit can stop editing tools making changes to the Registry, prevent DOS-based software from running in a Windows DOS session and restarting the PC in DOS mode and there's a provision to only run designated Windows programs.

USING POLEDIT

Since Poledit makes changes to your PC's Registry files it's a very good idea to carry out a backup before you do anything else. Go to Run on the Start menu and type 'regedit' to open the Registry editor program. On the Registry menu select Export Registry file, select a name ('regbak' is customary) and a location and click OK. If after using Poledit you get any error messages relating to the Registry simply double click on your Regbak.reg file and it will automatically reinstall your backup.

The two versions of Poledit are in slightly different locations on the installation CD-ROMs. On the Windows 95 disk it can be found in D:\Admin\Apptools\Poledit; for Windows 98 look in D:\Tools\ Reskit\Netadmin\Poledit (where D: is the drive letter of your CD-ROM). Poledit wasn't included with Windows 95 on floppy disks, but it can be downloaded from the Microsoft website at:

http://www.microsoft.com/downloads/search.asp

the file is called Policy.exe.

Step one is to install the main Poledit files on your PC. Go to Add/ Remove Programs in Control Panel, select the Windows Setup tab and click Have Disk. Use the Browse button to navigate to the folder on the CD-ROM containing Poledit and select the file Poledit.inf. Click OK, select System Policy Edit then Install. A new item called System Policy

Editor will now appear in Start > Programs > Accessories > System Tools. By the way, the Windows CD-ROM must be in the drive every time you run Poledit.

You can also run Poledit directly from the CD-ROM, providing you don't later restrict the use of the Run command! Go to Run on the Start menu and use the Browse button to find your way to the Policy.exe file on the disk.

When you run the Windows 95 version of Poledit for the first time you will be prompted to open a file called 'admin.adm', click Open and the main System Policy screen appears. On the Windows 98 version you normally go straight to the opening screen. Next go to the File menu and select Open Registry then click on the Local User icon.

In Windows 95 you will see a set of sub-menus called Local User Properties detailing the areas of Windows that you can control, in Windows 98 click on the item Windows 98 System and a similar set of options should appear, though it will exclude the 'Network' controls, which are dealt with separately. The four items we are interested in, and common to both versions of Poledit, are called Shell, Control Panel, Desktop Display and Restrictions; we'll look at each one in turn (in the order that they appear in the Windows 98 version of Poledit).

Click on the plus sign next to Shell and two further sub-folders appear, Custom Folders and Restrictions. Click the plus sign again and the items you can control appear, with a checkbox alongside each one. There's not much to interest the average user in Custom Folders, it's mostly concerned with changing the default locations of programs, so we'll move swiftly on to Restrictions. This contains a set of options to remove or hide Windows user interface features. The ones most users with a shared PC might want to check are: 'Remove Run Command', 'Remove Folders from Settings on Start menu', 'Hide Drives in My Computer' and 'Don't Save Settings on Exit'. Most of the others are either concerned with network features or fairly extreme things, like disabling Shut Down or hiding all of the icons on the desktop.

On now to Control Panel, which opens with four or five options, depending on the version of Poledit. They are: Display, Network, Passwords, Printer and System. Clicking each item brings up a further set of options in the window below. It's worth checking everything in Display and System since these are the things that can cause the most problems through accidental and deliberate tampering. The restrictions you impose

Using Poledit to restrict access to key Windows
functions

in Network, Password and Printers will depend on what type of setup you
have and who uses the PC.

The next item is Desktop and there are just two restrictions here that
allow you to fix the wallpaper and colour scheme. Users can still make
changes but they will be reset to your defaults when the machine is restarted.

Finally Restrictions. This set of options prevents Registry editing tools
being used (including Poledit – so definitely leave this one alone!), stops
DOS programs running in a DOS window or restarting the PC in DOS

mode and lets you specify which programs are allowed to be used on your PC. It's worth disabling the DOS options especially if the PC is under threat from knowledgeable users. Imposing restrictions on which programs may be used is actually quite difficult to use since you have to specify the full path for each program and this can be quite a chore, it's easier to remove programs you won't allow, and disable the Run command or hide the drives.

After setting your restrictions exit Poledit and you will be asked to confirm that you want to make changes to the Registry, click OK. Some of them will occur immediately, others will take place the next time the PC is booted up.

RESCUE PLAN

Using Poledit/Restrictions to prevent editing the Registry stops Poledit working, so how can it be changed back again? The solution is to use Windows WordPad or a word processor to manually create a new Registry entry. Open a new document and enter the following text:

> REGEDIT4
> [HKEY_CURRENT_USER\Software\Microsoft\Windows\Current Version\Policies\Explorer]
> "RestrictRun"=dword:00000000
> [HKEY_CURRENT_USER\Software\Microsoft\Windows\Current Version\Policies\System]
> "DisableRegistryTools"=dword:00000000

Call the file 'recover.reg' and save it in the root directory of your PC's C: drive. Reboot the PC to DOS mode and at the prompt type: 'regedit recover.reg'. Restart and the restriction should be removed.

Q&A Real world problems

Locked out

Q   I have read that that most ten year olds can defeat the password features of Windows. As a seventy year old who put an easily remembered, since

forgotten, password on his taxation computations in Excel just to see what happens, is it possible to share the remedy and save several hours of work?
D.B. via e-mail

A   Let that be a lesson to you! Always write down your passwords and keep them in a safe place. There are many ways to disguise a set of passwords or PIN numbers, bogus phone numbers in an address book, simple scrambling – reversing the letter or number order – a diary entry using the letters to create a sentence, though of course you still have to remember how or where they're hidden. . .

Several companies specialise in recovering password-protected data and there are quite a few shareware programs that can also do the job. Most of them employ the 'brute force' method, which simply means they go through all the possible letter number combinations – several million per minute – until they stumble on the right one. You can find out more from the following websites:

http://www.passwordservice.com/faq.htm
http://www.elkraft.ntnu.no/~huse/xlpassword.htm
http://www.lostpassword.com/msofpass97.htm

Child's play

Q   On a computer at school, two children pressed reset at an obviously inopportune moment and now all the windows and displays in the screens as well as the mouse pointer are very large. The Windows screens in the start-up sequence are OK but once the Windows 95 desktop screen comes up it is huge so we only see a small amount of the screen.

I assume I need to do a change to the Settings window in the Display part of the Control Panel. I can get into this but cannot get down the window to do what I assume is the necessary change. Scrolling or page down has no effect. Am I right in my assumption and if so is there any way I can get down this screen? Is there another way of correcting the problem? Or do I have to reload Windows 95 and so lose all the work stored on the hard disk?
G.C. via e-mail

A   Even if you can't actually see the selections in Control Panel you can access them by pressing the down arrow on the keyboard, try them one at a time, pressing the Return key each time, until you get to the Display option. Alternatively restart the PC in Safe Mode by pressing the F8 key during the boot-up sequence. Windows will then load with 'standard' display setting and you'll be able to get into a normally sized Control Panel.

Lock out the Luddite

Q My business partner is a computer Luddite and frequently messes up his PC settings. Is there a way of locking Windows settings, or fixing it so that they are restored on re-booting?
J.W. via e-mail

A The simplest way to stop your partner's tinkering is to hide or restrict access to the Windows Control Panel. If you are using Windows 98 (version 1) then install Tweak UI; it's on the Win 98 CD-ROM, Tools > Reskit > Powertoy, right-click on tweakui.inf and select Install. The Tweak UI icon appears in Control Panel, select the Control Panel tab and disable all of the components, or just the ones your partner interferes with. (Unfortunately this facility is only on the Windows 98 version of Tweak UI.) There are also a number of utilities that will restrict access to programs and Windows components, including the Control Panel. Have a look at Sentry 98 and Security Administrator, shareware/trial versions can be downloaded from:

http://www.sentry98.com

and

http://www.softheap.com/secagent.html

Beat the bin

Q How do I recover files that I have foolishly placed in the Recycle Bin – then emptied. . .? Is this possible?
G.S. via e-mail

A It is possible, with certain provisos, but to stop it happening again always leave it for a day or two before you empty the Recycle Bin. OK lecture over. When you delete something in Windows all you are actually doing is removing the reference to the file or program from the filing system, the data remains on the disk but the space it occupies is marked as free, so it will eventually be overwritten. Various utilities are available that allow you to recover deleted files. One of the easiest to use is Recover 4All; a shareware version that is limited to files up to 10kb is available from most shareware sites, including Tucows at:

http://tucows.mirror.ac.uk/adnload/dlrec4all95.html

Shredded evidence

Q   Since files sent to the Recycle Bin are not actually deleted, until they are overwritten, is it possible to permanently delete possibly highly confidential files?
T.N. via e-mail

A   You'll find a selection of file shredders at shareware sites like www.tucows.com and www.jumbo.com. However, even that may not be enough to completely remove all traces; security services and the military routinely destroy the hard disk drives on scrap and redundant computers, just to make sure. . .

Junior meddlers

Q   I am having a problem with children at school moving the taskbar to the edges of the screen. We want to lock them into position at the base of the screen – the taskbar, not the children! What can you suggest apart from keep moving it back to the bottom when the little Herbets have messed around with it?
A.J. via e-mail

A   A shareware program called IconLock stores icon and desktop settings, so they can be easily restored if someone tinkers with them. Alternatively the icons and the Taskbar can be locked and password protected; everything still works normally but no changes can be made. The 'zip' file is just under 900kbs and can be downloaded from:

http://www.zdnet.com/pcmag/pctech/content/18/14/ut1814.002.html

CHAPTER 9

Viruses, worms and Trojans

Conspiracy theorists have a field day after every PC and e-mail virus outbreak. Everyone from anti-virus software manufacturers drumming up business to the FBI and dark forces within the music industry has been blamed for spreading them. But wherever they come from, the bottom line is that your PC is under attack!

RESIST INFECTION

The main target for viruses is Windows 95 and 98 PC owners and in particular those using Outlook and Outlook Express e-mail. In adding extra functionality to these programs Microsoft has inadvertently created a number of security loopholes that virus writers have been quick to exploit.

However, providing you take sensible precautions, the chances of being infected are relatively small. In this chapter we'll look at some simple commonsense measures you can take to protect your PC and the data stored on it. Most viruses have clearly identifiable behaviour patterns or 'signatures' that anti-virus software can be programmed to recognise. If you haven't got a virus 'scanner' on your PC you are just asking for trouble – get one now, and make sure you regularly back up all non-replaceable data. The effectiveness of anti-virus programs depends entirely on how often you update the software. It's no good hoping that the freebie anti-virus software that was loaded on your machine when you brought it will protect you; it was out of date long before you got the computer home!

An estimated 300 new viruses are created each week and as events have shown they can spread like wildfire. In May 2000 the 'ILOVEYOU' or 'Love Bug' virus infected several million PCs and systems around the world in a matter of hours; anti-virus software companies respond quickly but it can still take them several days to come up with countermeasures and make them available to users.

The damage caused by viruses varies enormously and the good news is that most are relatively harmless or benign. If you receive a lot of e-mail you may have one or two infecting your machine without you knowing it, even if you follow the very sensible advice about not opening unsolicited e-mail attachments. E-mail viruses, or 'worms' can get into your machine just by opening a message and this can be a very serious problem if you are using an older version of Outlook Express 4 and 5 and haven't downloaded the self-installing security patch which can be found at:

http://www.microsoft.com/technet/security/bulletin/ms99-032.asp

Click the following link to start the download:

ftp://ftp.microsoft.com/peropsys/IE/IE-Public/Fixes/usa/Eyedog-fix/ x86/q240308.exe

This will protect you against the many variations of the 'BubbleBoy' Java Script worm, which was released in 2000 and continues to proliferate under a variety of different names. Fortunately it rarely damages files but it is self-replicating and will attach itself to e-mails sent by you to others. One of the most virulent strains is known as 'Kak'. If your PC or e-mail program has been behaving oddly recently, unusual 'Driver memory' and 'Registry error' messages have been appearing on the screen, you've lost the ability to print e-mails from within Outlook Express or the PC switches itself off for no apparent reason, then Kak or one of its cousins is a prime suspect. There are also suggestions there's a version that affects Netscape Messenger though we have yet to see any hard evidence of this.

If you think you have been infected don't despair, it's fairly easy to remove the files from your machine, you'll find full instructions and more details about the worm on the following websites:

http://www.datafellows.com/v-descs/kak.htm
http://vil.mcafee.com/dispVirus.asp?virus.k=10509
http://www.symantec.com/avcenter/venc/data/wscript.kakworm.html

The trouble is a worm like Kak can be sent to you quite innocently inside an e-mail from someone you know and trust. Simply reading the message activates the worm and the first you know about it is an error message or an on-screen prompt asking you if you want to run an 'ActiveX Script', but by that time it's too late. Once the patch is installed you will see ActiveX

If you see this warning message it is possible that the e-mail
you have just received contains a worm

warning messages if you receive an infected e-mail; don't worry, it can no
longer damage your machine, just make sure you alert the sender.

The infamous ILOVEYOU virus, also known as the 'Love Bug' and the
'Killer from Manilla' makes use of another Windows feature called Visual
Basic Script. Unlike BubbleBoy and Kak this one gets into your PC via an
e-mail attachment with the extension *.vbs. It can do nothing unless the
attachment is opened, so NEVER open attachments unless you are
absolutely sure they are safe! If you are in any doubt delete it and contact
the sender.

News of the Love Bug virus spread quickly and most PC users were on
the alert for bogus messages of affection, but within days of the original
outbreak the code had been modified and there are now dozens of variations,
riding on the back of e-mail attachments with plausible headers, like 'Check
this out', 'Very Important Please Read' and so on. It takes a great deal of self-
control not to open an attachment with an innocuous or intriguing message,
especially if a friend or colleague has sent it.

The latest anti-virus updates should be able to identify and disinfect most
strains of the Love Bug but you can reduce your chances of being infected,
or if it does, stop you passing it on to others by disabling the Visual Basic
Script feature in Windows 95 and 98 (the loophole has been removed from
Windows ME). It's unlikely to cause any problems if you're using a stand-
alone machine running standard office type applications. The procedure is
very simple, in Windows 98 open Control Panel (Start > Settings) double-
click on the Add/Remove Programs icon and select the Windows Setup tab.
Double click on Accessories and scroll down the list to Windows Scripting
Host, deselect the check box and click OK. In Windows 95 open My
Computer, go to the View menu, select Options and the File Types tab.

Scroll down the list to find 'VBScript Script File', click Remove and in the confirmation dialogue box that appears select Yes. For more information on current virus infestations have a look at:

http://www.symantec.com/avcenter/index.html

Prevent infections like the ILOVEYOU virus by switching off Windows Scripting Host

TROJANS

Viruses are bad enough but here's something else for you to worry about the next time you're on-line. When you are connected to the Internet it is possible for others to gain access to your PC, read files, scan your address book, see which sites you've been visiting, steal passwords, download files and viruses onto your machine, even wipe your disk, and you won't know a thing about it!

Fortunately for most users the risk of it happening is quite small; nevertheless the possibility exists, and in the future when we are using 'always-on' and broadband connections to the net, like DSL and cable modems, this kind of snooping could turn into a real threat.

This is how it works. Typically a program called a 'Trojan', which gets onto the PC as an e-mail attachment, or is deliberately planted by someone with access to the machine, opens an unauthorised 'backdoor' into the computer's hard disk. Once there it remains hidden but will activate whenever you go on-line, and provide anyone with the necessary 'Client' program full remote access to your machine.

If you connect to the Internet by a normal 'dial-up' telephone line connection you are protected to some extent by the fact that your PC is relatively anonymous. When you go on-line most Internet Service Providers (ISPs) assign a 'dynamic IP' address to your PC, which changes every time you log on. This makes it difficult, but not impossible, for anyone deliberately to target your computer. Some client programs randomly trawl through IP addresses for infected PCs but some Trojans automatically report back to the sender your current IP address as soon as you go on line.

Unlike a conventional virus or worm, Trojans are not necessarily destructive, which makes them hard to detect. Most of the top virus scanners – if regularly updated – will find the commonest Trojans, which for the record have names or go under file and program aliases like Back Orifice, Netbus, Buddylist, Deep-Throat, Girlfriend and Winsaver. If you feel you may be under threat you might like to try this rough and ready Trojan detector, which looks for programs that configure your PC to 'listen' for an Internet connection; be warned that it is really only suitable for stand-alone, non-networked PCs.

Here's what to do: switch off and re-boot your PC. This is important because any running programs or previous Internet connections since Windows was booted will give spurious results. Next, open an MS-DOS window (Start > Programs > MS-DOS) and type the following command at the flashing prompt:

netstat –an >>c:\netstat.txt

Press Return then type 'exit' then Return and the MS-DOS window will disappear. Now open Windows Explorer and in the root directory of your C: drive there will be a newly created file called Netstat.txt. Double click on it and it should open automatically with Windows Notepad. If you see any numbers and entries, don't panic; it could all be quite innocent but it should put you on your guard and you might want to investigate further.

Even if this simple test suggests that our PC is currently Trojan-free that's no reason to be complacent and you still might be infected in the future. In addition to all of the usual commonsense precautions, including not opening suspicious and unexpected e-mail attachments, you should install software that prevents anyone from remotely accessing your PC. This type of program is commonly called a 'Firewall', and there are plenty to choose from, but far and away the best and most popular one is ZoneAlarm, and the good news is that for personal and non-commercial use it's completely free. The file is just over 1.6Mb so it should only take a few minutes to download from:

www.zonelabs.com

ZoneAlarm is very easy to set up and use and can be set to start automatically when you boot your PC. It operates in the background, monitoring programs that you have given permission to connect to the Internet; if a program unexpectedly tries to open a connection without your say so you will be warned. ZoneAlarm checks incoming e-mail for 'Love Bug' type worms but the most interesting feature is the one that alerts you when any attempt is made to gain access to your PC. What surprises a lot of users is how frequently this happens; you might get two or three warnings in a half hour session. Usually most alerts are entirely innocent and are often nothing more sinister than delayed Internet site responses, if you're tired of waiting for a page to download, or sites calling the previous user of your current IP address. ZoneAlarm blocks all intrusions, displays the IP address of the site trying to get through and gives you the option to find out who it is.

In the case of an actual attack ZoneAlarm is unlikely to tell you very much or identify the would-be intruder as any serious hacker will know enough to cover their tracks. However, it's worth trying a program called Neo Trace – a trial version can be downloaded from:

http://www.pkware.com/catalog/neotrace.html

Firewall programs like ZoneAlarm can protect your
PC against intruders

which, in the manner of all good Hollywood spy movies, plots the path of
the connection between you and the suspect address on a map of the world,
with accompanying sound effects.

If you want to give yourself a really nasty shock there's an excellent
Internet site that automatically tests the integrity of your machine and its
defences – or lack of them ... With your permission it simulates the kind
of surreptitious backdoor snooping an intruder might use to gain access to
your system. The utility is called Shields Up! It was created by Steve Gibson

of Gibson Research. It's free to use and it can be found at:

http://grc.com

If that doesn't convince you of the need for a Firewall on your PC, nothing will!

Q&A Real world problems

Nasty infection

Q   At start-up I receive the toolbar message 'Driver Memory Error' followed by a screen warning saying 'Registry Editor – Cannot import C:\Windows\kak.reg'. I have tried Scandisk to no avail. One suggestion from Compaq was that it was a program that needed uninstalling. I have hunted through Add/Remove programmes but found no odd ones. There is no indication from the message what file it could be. In any event, how does this affect the memory, what is a kak.reg file and how do I solve it?
R.A. via e-mail

And . . .

Q   For some months now every time I switch on my PC it creates the attached empty file KAK.HTA and opens it on the desktop. I delete it from the Start-up folder and the Recycle Bin but it just keeps being recreated. This is presumably as a result of the lines of code in my autoexec file. Does this code serve any useful purpose? My highly computer-literate son denies putting it there. Could it be the result of something one of us downloaded? It doesn't seem to do any harm; it's just a small annoyance. Any advice?
D.B. via e-mail

And . . .

Q   Now and again this strange error message appears on the desktop. If I click OK the thing shuts down and restarts. The message is: 'Kagou-Anti-Kro$oft says not today'. It only appears now and again otherwise everything seems okay.
K.L. via e-mail

A   This virus just won't go away and continues to create a considerable number of problems for users of older versions of Outlook Express. To summarise, Kak apparently originated in France, is carried on e-mails and affects MS Outlook and Outlook Express versions 4 and 5. There have also been reports of a version that affects Netscape Messenger. You only have to read the message for the infection to occur. You may see a dialogue box asking if you want to run 'Active X' scripts but usually the first symptom is an error message usually something like 'S3 Memory allocation failed'. You will probably find you can't print e-mail messages and the PC may suddenly switch itself off for no apparent reason.

Don't panic, it won't affect the rest of your system and removal is fairly straightforward. Kak creates several files in the root directory of the C: drive and other locations, and creates a new Registry entry. These must all be removed, and to prevent the virus spreading to others, the option to add a Signature to outgoing e-mails must be disabled in Outlook Express. When that's done install the patch from the Microsoft web site at:

http://www.microsoft.com/technet/security/bulletin/ms99-032.asp

and click the link

ftp://ftp.microsoft.com/peropsys/IE/IE-Public/Fixes/usa/Eyedog-fix/x86/q240308.exe

That will take you direct to the patch download; follow the instructions to install it automatically. Don't worry about the name 'Eyedog', Kak is one of a family of viruses (that started life as 'Bubbleboy') that exploit the same loophole in MS Outlook. If you receive an infected e-mail after you've disinfected your PC you will get an Active X warning message, it can't do any damage; however you should contact the sender to let them know that they are infected. Finally, if you are using a virus scanner make sure it is up to date.

However, there are many different variants of kak, which plant files in different locations and anti-virus software updates may not be programmed to seek them all out. If you continue to get odd 'kak related' messages try a manual search using Find on the Start menu, to look for files with the extension *.hta and *.kak and delete them all. If you're familiar with the Registry you should also check that the following key has been purged:

HKEY_LOCAL_MACHINE\SOFTWARE\Microsoft\Windows\CurrentVersion\Run\cAg0u

A plage on your PC

Q   I recently had to kill a virus caught by Norton Anti-Virus software. Now when I start up the PC (Windows 98) I get error messages about a file called 'Inetd.exe'. I have tried to find the missing file in my Windows disk without success. These messages are very annoying! Any ideas?
E.G. via e-mail

A   You have been infected by a nasty little e-mail worm called Plage. Amongst other things it modifies the Windows system file win.ini, which it appears your anti-virus software may have missed. Full instructions on how to manually delete this intruder can be found at:

http://www.fireantivirus.com/virusinfo/library/plage.htm

False alarm

Q   I have been plagued by what looks like a virus message on my screen for sometime now about a file called 'ptsnoop.exe', but I haven't seen it mentioned anywhere, is it dangerous?
D.W. via e-mail

A   Ptsnoop is not a worm or virus but a modem diagnostic utility that checks the modem driver when a COM port is opened. It doesn't do any harm and it can be safely disabled as follows: Start > Programs > Accessories > System Tools > System Information, go to the Tools menu then System Configuration, Start up tab and uncheck the item 'ptsnoop.exe'. If you experience any problems switch it back on again.

CHAPTER 10

Preventative maintenance

*A few minutes spent on preventative maintenance
now could save you from a potentially disastrous
failure in the future. It's high time you cleaned your
PC's hardware and software!*

CLEAN THE MACHINE

A clean PC is a happy PC but dirt and dust are not just unsightly, they can do real damage. Forget expensive air purifiers, your PC does an admirable job of extracting dust and particles from the atmosphere. After only a few months the insides of most desktop PCs are coated with a thick layer of dust and debris sucked into the casing by the cooling fan. Most of it is relatively harmless but if it gets onto the recording and replay heads in the floppy drive or onto the optical pickup in the CD-ROM drive it can cause problems. Accumulations of dust in the power supply can also lead to overheating and in extreme cases, failure.

Dirt, hairs and gunge find their way into that highly effective desktop vacuum cleaner, otherwise known as your mouse, making pointer movement erratic. PC keyboards really should have removable crumb trays since most of us are messy eaters. Then there's your printer; dust and fibres from paper clogs inkjet nozzles and the feed mechanism, eventually it can lead to paper jam and mis-feed and if you've got a scanner the chances are the glass platen is covered in greasy finger marks.

Before you start make sure your PC is properly switched off and not in standby or sleep mode. If you're concerned switch it off at the mains, but leave it plugged in so the case remains earthed. After each cleaning job it's a good idea to boot the machine up and make sure it is behaving normally, that way if a problem occurs you'll know where to start looking.

We'll begin with the mouse. You can muck out most models by turning them upside down; remove the ball retaining plate by twisting it a quarter of a turn anticlockwise. Take the ball out, shake and blow out any loose debris.

Erratic pointer movement is almost always caused by a build-up of grime encrusting the movement rollers. This can be easily removed with a cocktail stick or sharpened matchstick, blow it out again and reassemble. Give the outside a wipe over with a damp cloth.

Next it's the turn of the crumb-catcher or keyboard. Flip it upside down and give it a shake to dislodge the bigger bits lodged between and behind the keys. However, the best way to clean it is to use an 'air duster', which can be bought from your local PC or stationery store for around a fiver. Basically it's a can of compressed air or non-toxic gas, with a long thin nozzle that can get in between the keys, and blast out the remnants of a hundred coffee breaks and lunches. You can also try sucking out the gunge with a vacuum cleaner, incidentally you can get miniature battery powered models for this kind of job but they're not very powerful. You can clean the keys with a lightly moistened cloth and a dab of washing up liquid. If any water drips into the innards – and this applies to any of the parts you are cleaning – it's best not to switch the PC back on but leave the affected component overnight in a warm place.

Now for the system unit (and if you don't feel confident about poking inside your computer you should skip this step). Before you remove the lid remember to switch the PC off at the mains socket and remove the plug from the socket. It's a good idea to touch the metal case before you start, to dispel any static charge that may have built up on your clothing and body. The golden rule when working inside your PC is don't touch anything unless you know what you are doing, and blow, don't suck! In other words, don't shove the nozzle of your vacuum cleaner's extension hose inside the box. Use an air duster to remove the layer of dust drawn into the case by the cooling fans. Pay particular attention to the areas around the main processor, its cooling fan and fins which can get clogged with dust. Get into all of the corners and save a good long puff for the back of the metal box housing the power supply.

This step is optional but if you are familiar with your PC's innards, before you put the lid back on give the plugs and sockets going to the motherboards and disk drives a gentle push, to make sure they're properly seated. All of the components inside a PC are subjected to repeated heating and cooling cycles as the machine is switched on and off, and this can lead to an effect known as 'contact creep' whereby plugs and microchips gradually work their way loose from their sockets. When you have finished replace the lid, switch on and make sure everything is working properly.

Back now to the outside. It's worth treating the floppy and CD-ROM drive to a run through with disk cleaning kits, always buy good quality items from reputable suppliers and always follow the instructions, especially with 'wet' cleaners that use an alcohol cleaning fluid. Allow the fluid plenty of time to evaporate before using the drive. Reseating all of the plugs and sockets on the back panel is a good idea too, though make sure you know where they all go; if necessary label the cables or draw a simple diagram first, before you disconnect anything. Give the whole case a wipe over with a lightly moistened cloth and some washing up liquid to remove the finger marks, especially around the disk slots and switches. While you're at it give the outside of the monitor a wipe over and clean the screen with an anti-static cleaner wipe or a dab of window cleaner liquid on a soft cloth.

The high voltages flying around inside CRT-based monitors produce a powerful static electrical charge that works like a magnet on dust and airborne particles. The screen will probably need a thorough clean, especially if there are any smokers nearby as their exhalations leave a particularly sticky residue. Use one of the specially made screen cleaners as these usually contain anti-static agents that slow down the build-up of dirt. Remove all of the clutter from the top of the monitor, it might be blocking ventilation holes, which could cause problems. Give the vents a quick blast with your air duster and clean the outside of the case with your damp soapy cloth. LCD viewing screens are generally a lot easier to deal with, they run fairly cool and do not attract dust to anything like the same extent as CRT monitors so a quick wash and brush up is usually all that's needed.

Printers are best dealt with using the air duster; if possible open the top or front so you can get a good shot at the rollers and paper path. On inkjet models avoid blowing near to the ink cartridges, better still take them out first but keep the air jet away from any ink ports or tubes, it can be incredibly messy, and it probably doesn't do it any good either! Wipe the outer casing and it's done. Scanners don't usually get very dirty, though the platen is often dotted with greasy finger marks, so give that the once-over with a glass cleaner or a screen wipe.

SPRUCE UP YOUR SOFTWARE

So much for the hardware, but your hard disk drive will also benefit from a spot of spring cleaning, which should make your system run faster and less prone to crashes.

Before you begin make sure that all of your backups are up to date, just in case. Start by removing any programs that you no longer use, especially all those demos and magazine cover disk freebies. Ideally you will have an uninstaller program on your PC, like CleanSweep, WinDelete, etc., which monitors each installation so it can be completely removed. If not get one, they're a real investment and used properly they'll keep your PC hard disk drive running smoothly. Otherwise you will have to use Add/Remove Programs in Control Panel or the application's own uninstaller utility – if it has one – which you may find listed alongside the application on the Start > Programs list, or in the application's folder when opened in Windows Explorer. Never remove programs by deleting files in Windows Explorer or you will regret it! Remove only one program at a time and restart the PC each time, watching out for any error messages during the re-boot.

If a problem occurs try reinstalling the last program you've deleted. You may find that some desktop shortcuts remain; they can be deleted by right clicking on them. Some programs may still be listed in Add/Remove programs. It does no harm but they can be zapped with the Windows user's friend Tweak UI (or the Registry tweak outlined in Chapter 6). It is included on the first release of the Windows 98 CD-ROM (Tools > Reskit > PowerToy). The Windows 95 version can be downloaded from the Microsoft website at:

http://www.microsoft.com/windows95/downloads/contents/
WUToys/W95PwrToysSet/Default.asp

Windows 98 and ME have their own rudimentary disk cleaner utilities. Go to Start > Programs > System Tools > Disc Cleanup and click OK to select Drive C. Select the Disk Cleanup tab. This will give you the option to empty Recycle Bin and folders that Windows and your Internet browser uses to temporarily store information. If you've upgraded from Windows 95 make a point of selecting the item 'Windows 98 Uninstall Information' as this can recover up to 80Mb of wasted hard disk space. This is supposed to let you revert to Windows 95, but if you upgraded to the FAT 32 filing system (as you should have done) then it no longer serves any purpose since it is impossible to go back.

If you are using Windows 95 you'll have to clear out those Temporary folders manually. Shut down all running applications and use Explorer to open Windows and look for a folder called Temp or Temporary. You can safely delete all files with the extension *.tmp, anything you're not

Disk Cleanup for (C:)   [?] [X]

Disk Cleanup | More Options | Settings |

You can use Disk Cleanup to free up to 19.98 MB of disk space on (C:).

Files to delete:

☑ 🔒 Temporary Internet Files   9.27 MB
☐ 📄 Downloaded Program Files   0.00 MB
☐ 🗑 Recycle Bin   0.44 MB
☐ 📁 Old ScanDisk files in the root folder   9.91 MB
☑ 📁 Temporary files   0.35 MB

Total amount of disk space you gain: 9.63 MB

─ Description ─────────────────────────────────────
The Temporary Internet Files folder contains Web pages stored on your hard disk for quick viewing. Your personalized settings for Web pages will be left intact.

                                    [View Files]

                    [OK   ]   [Cancel]

The disk cleanup utility in Windows 98 and ME can remove unwanted clutter

absolutely sure about leave alone. Remember, one step at a time, so carry out another shut down and re-boot to make sure you haven't removed anything vital. If something does go wrong you can use Undo Delete in Recycle Bin.

Temporary Internet files can be emptied from within Internet Explorer. Go to the View or Tools menu (depending which version you are using) and select Internet Options. On the General tab look for the item Temporary Internet Files and click on Delete; while you are there you can reduce the amount of space used by clicking on Settings and moving the slider to the left – 100Mb is about right unless you rely on cached Internet pages. Personally I'm happy to clear this folder out completely, including cookies, little files that contain information about sites you've visited. You can do this from Windows Explorer. If you want to keep any, for sites that you visit frequently, or may contain passwords, etc., click Select All on Explorer's Edit menu hold down the Ctrl key and work your way down the list and deselect those you're not certain about or want to keep, then click on Delete.

Now for all those e-mail messages. On Outlook Express the option to 'compact' all of the messages in your inbox and outbox folders, to free up

The maintenance option in Outlook Express can free
up space used by e-mails

some space, is on the File menu under Folder. If you want to make a clean start you can use Select All on the Edit menu and hold down Ctrl to deselect any that you want to hang on to. Don't forget to right-click on the Deleted Items folder and select Empty Folder to remove the files to make the freed up space available.

To get your hard disk filing system back into shape you should run the Windows disk defragmenter or 'Defrag' utility: in fact you should be doing that at least once a month, weekly if the PC is in daily use and you do a lot of web browsing or regularly download material. Fortunately it's never too late to start, but before you run Defrag get into the habit of shutting down all running programs, empty the Recycle bin, disable power management and switch off any screensavers and anti virus software. The latter can usually be disabled from the System Tray (next to the clock) right-click on the icon and select Exit or Shutdown. If any programs are left running in the background and they access the hard disk, Defrag will be forced to restart and it'll never finish the job. To maximise the space on your hard disk empty your web browser's cache (in Internet Explorer click on Internet Options on the Tools menu, select the General tab and click Delete Files). When you've done that run the Scandisk utility which can be found by clicking Start > Programs > Accessories > System Tools.

Now you are ready to defrag. There are actually several versions of Defrag, the best one can be found alongside Scandisk in System Tools in the Accessories folder. This one has the option to optimise your hard disk's file structure by grouping the most frequently used programs together. (When Defrag opens, click the Settings button and check the item 'Rearrange files so my programs start faster'.) There's another slightly faster but less thorough version available from My Computer (right-click drive C:/ and select Properties and the Tools tab). If you are using Windows 98 and either of these two versions consistently 'hang' (and you've switched off all running programs) then try this. Insert your Windows 98 CD-ROM, if it starts automatically click on 'Browse this CD', otherwise use Windows Explorer to open the disk and work your way to the Tools and Mtsutil folders, right-click on Defrag.inf and select Install. Exit and re-boot, Defrag will run and give your PC's filing system a really comprehensive once-over.

Now that your PC's filing system is in apple-pie order it's time to clean up the Registry. Every time you install new software or make any changes to the way Windows or your programs work and look, it's entered in the Registry; however, when you delete programs redundant Registry entries

Windows disk defragmenter gives you the option to organise
your disk drive's filing system to make it more efficient

are often left behind and can sometimes cause conflicts. There is a basic
Registry checker utility in Windows (Start > Programs > Accessories >
System Tools > System Information, select Registry Checker on the Tools
menu) but it's only going to find the most serious faults. For a more in depth
check you should use a Registry Cleaner, Microsoft has one, called
RegClean which you can download from its website at:

http://support.microsoft.com/support/kb/articles/Q147/7/69.asp

RegClean will fix most common problems, but there is an even better third-
party alternative called RegCleaner. This excellent freeware program
automatically identifies redundant and corrupt entries and lets you manually
decide which ones to delete. It also backs up any changes, so they can be
undone, if anything unfortunate happens. You can download RegCleaner
from:

http://www.jv16.org

it's less than 500kb in size so it should only take a few minutes. It's self-
extracting, so click on the downloaded file and follow the instructions.

Regcleaner identifies redundant and corrupt Registry entries for
safe deletion

Before you run RegClean, or do anything to the Registry it's wise to
make a backup. You can do this by going to Run on the Start menu, type
in 'regedit' (without the inverted commas). When the Registry Editor
opens go to the Registry menu and click on Export Registry File, select a
location where you will know to find it, call the file regbak and click Save. If
anything goes wrong simply double-click on your newly created
'regbak.reg' file and the Registry will be restored automatically.

THE POWER TO PROTECT

No matter how carefully you treat your PC it is still at the mercy of outside
influences, and ones that you certainly should protect your machine against
are power cuts and voltage surges. Even a brief interruption in the mains
supply lasting no more than a split second can be enough to cause the files
and data you are working on to be lost, or worse! Important system files can
be corrupted and you'll be left with an inoperable PC.

We have become accustomed to a reliable mains supply in this country. For most of us living in towns and cities blackouts and 'brownouts' have been a comparatively rare occurrence in recent years and this has given us a false sense of security.

Power supply modules inside desktop PCs have improved enormously in the past few years and they can iron out minor variations in mains voltage and even cope with small 'spikes' and surges lasting a few milliseconds but a complete power loss can cause considerable damage. There is only one solution – other than using a battery-powered laptop – and that's a box of tricks called a UPS or uninterruptible power supply.

A UPS connects between the mains socket and your PC. Inside there's a re-chargeable battery, a battery charger and a circuit called an inverter. Its job is to convert the low voltage DC from the battery into 240 volts AC. When the mains fails the UPS switches automatically to the battery supply, maintaining the supply to the PC. Depending on the size of the battery the backup power supply can last from a few minutes to an hour or more, which should be long enough for you to save files, close programs and carry out a safe shut down.

Broadly speaking there are two types of UPS, on-line and standby. On-line models operate all of the time by keeping the battery constantly charged and supplying power to the inverter, which powers the PC. In this case the battery acts as a buffer between the PC and the mains, eliminating any irregularities in the mains voltage. Standby models kick in the instant the supply fails, taking between 2 and 10 milliseconds to restore power. The interruption is too brief to upset most modern PCs though it could cause problems on some older models. Incidentally, standby UPS tend to be a little cheaper than on-line types. Some more recent UPS designs are in effect hybrids, using what's known as a double conversion process, which lightens the load on the battery and provides a constant supply.

Most UPS modules are supplied with operating software that flashes up an on-screen warning when the mains supply fails. Some programs will carry out an automatic save and shutdown routine for you, in case you are not there to do it yourself. UPS management programs can also monitor the health of the battery, indicating when it needs replacing (usually every two to three years) and continually check the condition of the mains supply, logging trends and predicting possible failures. Most models now have a 'hot-swap' facility that allows the battery to be exchanged whilst the unit is operating. Additionally all UPS devices filter and 'condition' the mains voltage, removing potentially harmful spikes and surges, maintaining a steady smooth supply.

It all sounds terribly complicated and expensive but surprisingly it's not. UPS units designed to protect stand-alone Windows desktop PCs cost less than £100, which is a very small sum to pay when you consider how much your data, or even your computer is worth. UPS systems are normally rated by capacity quoted as volt-amperes or 'VA'. The typical range is from 200 to 1500VA. Heavy-duty UPS systems for servers and networks, fed from high-power circuits, go from 2000VA upwards. However for most home PC users UPS modules in the range 200 to 500VA are usually more than adequate, providing between 5 and 15 minutes worth of power, depending on the PC, size of monitor and any peripherals.

Q&A **Real world problems**

Windows cleaner

Q   I have a 68Mb file sitting on my hard drive called winundo.dat, which I think was created a few months ago when I upgraded from Windows 95 to 98. Windows 98 has been running fine since the upgrade – do you think it'll be okay to delete the file?
A.B. via e-mail

A   That file is just wasting valuable space, moreover if you changed to the FAT 32 filing system when you upgraded to Windows 98 you can't go back to Windows 95 anyway (and if you didn't change to FAT 32 you should do so, see Windows Help). However, rather than delete the file manually you should use the Windows 98 cleanup utility. Go to the Start menu and click Programs then Accessories > System Tools > Disk Cleanup. Drive C should appear in the dialogue box, click OK and the Disk Cleanup window appears. Select the Disk Cleanup tab and scroll down the list in the Files To Delete window looking for 'Delete Windows 98 uninstall information'. Click the checkbox and select OK.

Slipped disk

Q   The stainless steel sliding protective cover has become detached from a floppy disk in my A drive. The disk popped out as per normal, but left the metal cover inside. I have fiddled around gingerly not wanting to damage it, without success. Do you have any bright ideas as to how I may extract the errant cover?
F.B. via e-mail

A   You will have to dismantle the drive, or have an engineer look at it. If you try to extract the cover through the slot you'll almost certainly damage the mechanism or read/write heads. It's not a difficult job. Disconnect the PC from the mains socket, remove the lid and locate the drive. Observe the usual anti-static precautions; disconnect the power and data leads from the back of the drive. Note the polarity of the flat ribbon cable; one edge should be marked with a red stripe. The drive is normally held in place by four screws, two each side. Once they've been removed the drive should slide out through the front of the machine. The top panel on most floppy drives is held in place by indented clips, one on each corner. Gently prise the sides of the panel away from the chassis with a small screwdriver and the cover should come off and you'll be able to get at the innards. You may have to remove the front panel, this is also held in place by spring clips. If the drive is damaged it's not worth repairing; new ones can be bought for as little as £10.

The wrong track

Q   I recently purchased a new Pentium III PC. The 32x CD-ROM player gives no trouble when I use CD intensive applications such as Microsoft AutoRoute Express for Europe or games such as System Shock 2. The problem comes when I wish to play audio CDs. The tracks skip and jump and do everything but play normally. Do I need a new CD or is it the Windows Multimedia CD player at fault?
A.J. via e-mail

A   Try using a good quality CD/CD-ROM cleaner in the drive and make sure there are no marks or scratches on your audio CDs. It's unlikely to be a software fault but just to be on the safe side you could try removing and re-installing the CD player using Add/Remove Program in Control Panel.

Duo drive

Q I am going to add a CD-RW drive to my PC. Is there any reason why I wouldn't want to keep my existing CD drive, for example, to play music while I work on the new CD drive?
T.H. via e-mail

A You should keep the existing drive; indeed you will probably need it to install the driver and operating software on CD-ROM for your new CD-RW drive. In addition to playing music a second drive means you can leave a frequently accessed disk in one of the drives. Incidentally, only one drive can be used to play audio CDs, it will be the one with an audio connection to the PC's soundcard.

A wee problem

Q After my daughter and her friend had a little accident with a can of 7 Up and my PC keyboard, I decided to buy a cordless and mouseless keyboard. Can you explain to me why my cat has now urinated into two of these keyboards within the space of ten days? Both gave up the ghost, I have now had to resort to a normal keyboard and mouse. Could it be the infrared system is causing the cat to think it is now the local poo tray?
M.F. via e-mail

A Unless your present cat litter tray incorporates some kind of infra-red device it seems more likely the keyboard is emitting an odour that is either attractive or offensive to your cat, which is responding by marking its territory. You could try keeping the cat away from any new objects until they have acquired your smell. Another method is to stroke your cat around the chin area with a piece of cotton cloth then wipe the cloth on the new object, which makes it smell of the cat. You can also get cat repellent sprays and there is even a PC utility called PawSense, designed to keep cats off computer keyboards. It analyses key-press combinations and timings to determine when a cat climbs onto your keyboard. When a cat is detected, the utility plays a cat-annoying sound to repel the feline. More information is available at:

   http://www.bitboost.com/pawsense

Health monitor

Q I have a Gateway computer, which has been in constant use since I bought it four years ago. Over the last couple of months I have been experiencing problems with my monitor; the main problems are that the screen has become dim, it is slightly out of focus, making constant usage trying and the traditional Microsoft cloud wallpaper is now covered in swirls more like a contour map. In fact the blank page of a word document is also covered in swirls but this is not quite so noticeable.

I think degaussing might help but the monitor does not include this feature. Is there any other way to degauss it? If degaussing does not solve the problem, what will? Or should I save up for a new monitor?
E.D. via e-mail

A You monitor almost certainly does have a degaussing system but on a lot of older models it's an automatic function that de-magnetises the screen every time it is switched on. In any event it doesn't sound as though that's the problem with your monitor, stray magnetic fields show up as colour patches on an otherwise normal picture. The symptoms you describe are more likely to be caused by a failing picture tube or its drive circuitry. It's worth getting a repair estimate but if the tube is faulty it will almost certainly be cheaper to buy a new monitor. The cost of 14 and 15-inch models has fallen dramatically and prices start at under £100 from mail order companies advertising in computer magazines.

CHAPTER 11 **Finding solutions**

In an ideal world when your PC packs up, or starts behaving strangely, one phone call to the retailer or manufacturer's customer help line will resolve the problem, either with useful practical advice, or the promise of a visit from a service engineer that same day...

HELP IS AT HAND

It does actually happen sometimes and a lot of common problems can be fixed easily over the phone but what happens when the offer of free helpline assistance or guarantee has expired? Unless you have an extended warranty, service contract or a knowledgeable friend or relative on call, you're effectively on your own, or are you?

In fact there is more free (or nearly free) help on tap for dealing with computer problems than any other commercial product, you've just got to know where to look for it, and the right questions to ask. Unfortunately much of this help is only available if you have a working PC, or access to one with an Internet connection, which is a fat lot of good if your one and only PC has turned up its toes, you don't have the Internet, or the problem is you can't go on-line...

If you're not in an absolutely desperate hurry you can always write or fax a query to a newspaper or magazine problem page, though you should be aware that whilst most publications do their best they simply haven't got the space or facilities to answer every plea for help. PC agony aunts and uncles also tend to give precedence to the sort of problems that are likely to affect a lot of users in the hope that the solution will benefit the greatest number of readers. Obscure faults associated with a very particular combination of hardware and software are extremely difficult to diagnose at a distance and so stand a lesser chance of making it into print.

Keep all of the manuals and instruction books that came with your PC, peripherals and software in one place, so you can get at them easily. There are countless books on the subject, and the computing section in your local library and bookshops that tolerate browsers are also worth getting to know. It's a good idea to keep clippings of newspaper and magazine help pages as quite often you'll encounter a problem or fault that you vaguely remember reading about, why not start your own reference library? However, without doubt the fastest and most comprehensive source of help is the Internet.

Even if your PC is out for the count you can probably still go on-line using a friend's or relative's computer; publicly accessible PCs can also be found in schools and universities, libraries, motorway stations and Internet cafes or you could get an old Internet capable PC or laptop out of retirement; either way the net is your best and fastest hope of solving a problem.

There are many ways to use the Internet to get assistance, depending on the nature of the fault. Internet help falls into two broad categories: passive help, where the information you require is on a database somewhere and you have to look it up, and there's active help, where your problem is dealt with by a real person, or people and it's encouraging to know that there are lots of them out there in Internet land who give their time and expertise freely and unstintingly to help their fellow PC users.

If the problem occurred immediately after installing a new piece of hardware or software your first port of call should be the manufacturer's own website, to check whether there are any known problems or compatibility issues, drivers or patches to download and it's worth trawling through the site's FAQ sections. Many manufacturers' websites offer free on-line technical assistance and will reply by e-mail though the speed and reliability of these services varies enormously.

A surprisingly effective method for dealing with mysterious or obscure error messages that don't appear to relate to a specific item of software or hardware is to simply type the bones of the message into the Find field of one of the main Internet search engines. This often yields useful results; it's also very reassuring to know that you're not alone. . .

Any problem with Windows and you should head straight for the Microsoft Windows Troubleshooters, Knowledge Base and Error Message Resource Centre, the largest product database in existence. Unfortunately, whilst the answer to your Windows or Microsoft product-related problem is almost certainly buried in there somewhere, finding it is another matter.

There are two points of entry, try the 'Windows Troubleshooters' first at:

http://support.microsoft.com/support/tshoot/default.asp

for reasonably straightforward configuration and common error problems, and there is a helpful error message index for Windows 98 and ME which can be found at:

http://support.microsoft.com/support/windows/topics/errormsg/emresctr.asp

Otherwise go to the main Search page at:

http://search.microsoft.com/us/SearchMS25.asp

As you might expect it gets incredibly busy and you're often better off visiting the UK 'mirror' site at:

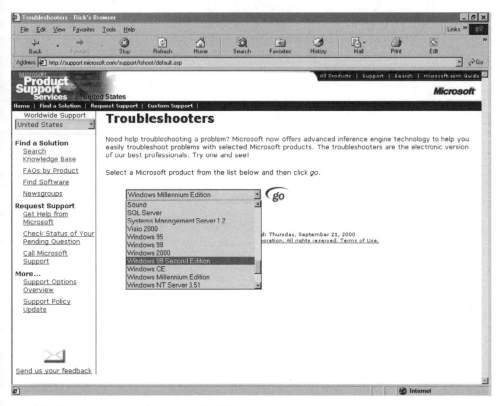

The Windows Troubleshooters on the Microsoft website is a
good place to start looking for solutions

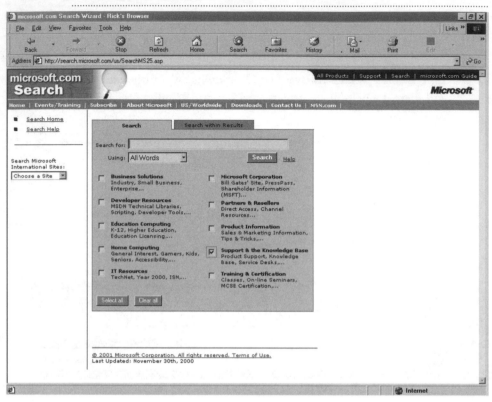

Search the Microsoft Knowledgebase for answers; just enter a
few simple keywords

http://search.microsoft.com/uk/SearchMS25.asp

Once there deselect everything except 'Support & the Knowledge Base' and
try searching just one or two keywords relating to your problem using the
'All Words' and 'Any Words' options first.

When it comes to seeking help from a real person then you have a
number of options. Posting your query on one of the many Newsgroups,
On-Line Conferences and Bulletin Boards can be a bit hit and miss. You
could get lucky and be inundated with replies within minutes, or hear
nothing for weeks, if ever. Generally speaking it's not something you can
easily get into from cold and is perhaps better suited to experienced users
who know the best places to ask for help.

Alternatively, try your luck with one of the many free on-line help
websites staffed by experts; again the quality of help can be a bit variable

and you may want to seek a second opinion before you do anything too drastic to your machine. Here's a small selection of sites to try to get you started:

http://www.allexperts.com
http://www.pchelponline.com
http://www.pchelplocator.com
http://www.myhelpdesk.com/computerhelp_wus.htm
http://www.freehelp.co.uk/support/swin98.htm
http://www.expertcity.com

ELEMENTARY HELP

There's a lot you can do to help yourself and your PC contains hidden features that can make fault finding a lot easier. Sherlock Holmes's worthy companion Dr Watson might seem like an odd choice of name for a little known Windows troubleshooting utility but like its namesake, its special talent is gathering evidence of foul deeds... In PC parlance they're known as general protection faults or GPFs, dastardly crimes committed by malevolent computer programs carrying out illegal operations that usually result in the dreaded 'blue screen of death'. Dr Watson is known in the trade as an application error debugger and it is designed to investigate problems, stepping in at the moment a crash occurs, making a detailed record of what your PC was up to at the time it happened.

Unlike other types of PC maintenance programs or tools Dr Watson cannot prevent a crash or help you to recover lost data, instead the information it collects can be used to diagnose, and occasionally indicate a solution to a recurrent software fault, and whilst the data it generates may not mean much to you, it can be sent to a manufacturer's technical support staff and the people who wrote the programs, to help them fix the problem or suggest a remedy. It can be especially useful on reproducible faults, where Windows or a program crashes after a particular sequence of events.

Microsoft has included Dr Watson in Windows since Version 3 but you're unlikely to have come across it, especially if you're using Windows 95, as it wasn't in all releases. However, it does appear in most versions of Windows NT and Windows 98 and ME. Part of the reason for its intermittent inclusion in Windows is that it has never been fully developed and can, in some circumstances, actually cause GPFs of its own; however, if you have a troublesome machine, and all else has failed, it is definitely worth trying.

The program is very well hidden in Windows 98 and ME, it can be found by going to Start > Programs > Accessories > System Tools > System Information, and you'll see it listed on the Tools menu. It's not enabled by default, so the first task is to get it up and running on your machine. The simplest method is to type 'drwatson.exe' (minus the quotation marks of course) in Run on the Start menu. Immediately you'll see a new icon pop up in the System Tray, next to the clock display on the Task Bar. However, it makes sense to have Dr Watson running in the background, constantly monitoring your PC. To do that you'll have to create a shortcut and include it in your Start-up folder so that it launches every time you boot up your machine.

It's quite straightforward, go to the Start button, select Programs, double-click on the Start-up icon and an Explorer window will open. Next, go to the File menu, select New then Shortcut and the Create Shortcut dialogue box opens. In the Command Line field type 'drwatson.exe', then Next, accept the default name and click on the Finish button. Alternatively

The Dr Watson report – this utility keeps a watchful eye on your
system and can help to identify problems

go to Start > Settings > Taskbar & Start Menu, select the Start Menu Programs tab. Click the Add button then Browse and find DrWatson.exe in the Windows folder, highlight and click Open, then Next. Now select the Start-up folder from the directory tree, click Next and Finish. In the unlikely event you experience any problems after Dr Watson has been installed simply highlight the icon in the Start-up folder and remove it by pressing the delete key.

From now on each time your machine suffers a GPF Dr Watson intercepts the crash and takes a 'snapshot' of your system. It identifies the program responsible and the nature of the fault and writes detailed technical information into a 'log' file (extension *.wlg) which is stored on your PC's hard disk (in the Dr Watson sub-folder in Windows). As an added bonus it gives you the opportunity to jot down a few notes of your own. This file can then be e-mailed to the technical support people, or printed out and sent by fax or letter.

When Dr Watson is running you can get an instant appraisal of your system by double-clicking on the icon in the System Tray, it takes a snapshot and a dialogue box appears on the screen in Standard view showing the Diagnosis window along with the jotter pad for your notes. This probably won't tell you much but if you then go to the View menu and select Advanced you'll see a row of tabs that provide much more detailed insights into your system, its configuration and the software it is running. If you prefer you can have Dr Watson always open in the Advanced view by selecting Options on the View menu and checking the box 'Open new windows in Advanced view'.

You can save this data by going to the File menu, select Save and use the Browse button to locate the Dr Watson folder in Windows, give the file a name (today's date for example) and click the Save button. It's worth doing this straight away, when your machine is operating normally as it will give you or anyone who's interested a benchmark to work from.

Dr Watson is not going to stop Windows from crashing (nothing will, if it's a mind to. . .) but the information it provides is a lot more useful than the normally meaningless error messages that appear and it just might help a software sleuth with their deductions.

CHAPTER 12

Boot camp – Top 100 tips

WINDOWS BUTTONS, KEYS AND ICONS

1. Help is always at hand! If you encounter a problem or get into difficulty, just press F1 and the associated Help file will be displayed. Swapping between open applications in Windows is easy; hold down the left 'Alt' key and press the 'tab' key. Pressing tab again steps through all of the programs the machine is currently running. If for any reason a program freezes, or the mouse stops moving try pressing 'Alt' and you may find that you can still select menus and options, using the four arrow cursor keys. If an application refuses to respond then press and hold down 'Ctrl', 'Alt' and 'Delete' in that order – once only – and the PC will display the Close Program window. This gives the opportunity to shut down the offending application, without having to exit Windows.

2. There are several Windows Explorer keyboard shortcuts worth remembering. Each time you press the Backspace key Explorer steps back one level up the directory tree. The F2 key allows you to rename a highlighted folder and Shift plus F10 brings up the context based pop-up menu. Clicking once or twice on the Size and Modified headings in the right hand 'Contents' window will sort the files in descending (i.e. largest files or most recently modified first) or ascending orders.

3. Here are some more Windows Explorer keyboard shortcuts. Pressing F4 displays the full contents of the Address/location panel, F5 refreshes the windows, updating any changes you may have made and F6 switches the focus between the various window 'panes'. Ctrl + A selects everything in the right hand window, Ctrl + Z undoes the last action and the Backspace key steps back through the parent directory tree. The asterisk key on the numeric keypad expands all of the directory branches whilst the '-' and '+' numeric keys collapse and expand the tree.

4. Windows Explorer sometimes seems to have a mind of its own and always seems to open with a different shape, position or icon and display settings. You can make it remember your preferences – for a while at least – set it up the way you want it to look then press Ctrl + Alt + Shift when you click on the close icon (the 'x' in the top right-hand corner). It will eventually forget but it's easy enough to repeat the exercise. It's a lot easier in Windows 98, set up Windows Explorer, go to the View Menu then Folder Options and select the View Tab and press the 'Like Current Folder' button.

5. If you have a Windows keyboard you obviously know the 'Windows' button (in between Ctrl and Alt keys) brings up the Start menu, but it can do a lot more besides. Win key (Wk) + D is a very quick way of getting to the desktop as it toggles maximise and minimise all windows. Wk + E opens Explorer, Wk + F opens Find, and Wk + R opens Run. System Properties opens with Wk + Pause, Wk + Tab steps through the programs on the Taskbar and Wk + F1 opens Windows Help.

6. There are several frequently-used multiple key shortcuts in Windows, like Ctrl + Alt + Del (to bring up the close program menu) and Alt + Tab (to switch between running applications) and dozens more in applications like Word, Excel and Outlook. Windows 95/98/2000 & ME has a nifty way to avoid two and three finger gymnastics, it's called 'Sticky Keys' and it's one of the Accessibility Options in Control Panel. It's aptly named because instead of pressing and holding a sequence of keys, you simply press each one in turn, your PC's internal speaker bleeps at you to confirm each key press. The facility can be easily switched on and off by pressing the shift key five times in quick succession.

Sticky Keys is not always installed by default, if you can't see the Accessibility Options icon in Control Panel click on Add/Remove in Control Panel, select the Windows tab then Accessibility and follow the instructions. To enable Sticky Keys open Accessibility Options and select the Keyboard tab, use the Settings button to change the way it behaves. Whilst you're there you might also like to switch on the Caps Lock bleeper, which also uses the PC's built-in speaker.

7. It doesn't take long for the Taskbar at the bottom of the screen to fill up with icons; they get smaller as the number increases and it can be difficult to read the labels. You can easily increase the size of the taskbar by moving the mouse pointer onto the top edge of the taskbar where it will turn into a vertical double-headed arrow. Click and hold the left mouse button and you can increase the width of the taskbar by dragging it upwards; it can be expanded to fill half of the screen if necessary. Clearly this takes up more room on the desktop, so make the Taskbar disappear, until it is needed. Click on the Start button, then Settings and Taskbar and check the Auto Hide option. From now on the Taskbar will only be shown when the mouse pointer is at the bottom of the screen.

8. The right mouse button in Windows has many hidden talents; here are a few to be getting on with. If you've got a lot of open windows and you want to get to the desktop, simply right click on the taskbar. This brings up a menu for minimising, tiling or cascading all windows; right click on the taskbar a second time to restore the windows. A right click on the recycle bin gives the option to empty it straight away. Disks can be quickly formatted by right-clicking on the disk drive icon in My Computer or Explorer.

9. The Start menu is a fast and easy way to launch frequently used programs, but you can make it work even quicker, and you don't even have to take your hands from the keyboard. Right-click on the Start button and select Open. A window appears, containing all of the Start menu icons. Insert a number (1, 2, 3, etc.) in front of the name of the applications you use most often. Click once on the icon and the name field turns blue. Wait a moment, click and click on the text and a cursor appears, then click again in front of the first letter of the name and type in the number. When you have finished close the window. Now you can launch the Start menu and a program by pressing the Windows 95 button on the keyboard, followed by the number. If you're using an older keyboard the shortcut is Ctrl + Esc, then the number.

10. You can do all sorts of clever things with the items on the Windows 98 Start menu. They can be copied, moved around and have their properties changed but the one thing you can't do is rename them, unless you have Internet Explorer 5.0 on your system. However, there is a way around that. You can change the name of an icon by left clicking on it and dragging it onto the desktop, it can then be renamed by clicking into the name field. Next, right-click on the newly named icon, drag it on to the Start button, put the mouse pointer where you want it to go on the Start menu, release the mouse button and choose 'Move Here' from the dialogue box that appears.

11. Every so often a program window opens in the wrong position or the menus and toolbars have disappeared off the top of the screen and you can't get them back. Here's a simple solution, press Alt + Spacebar to bring up the sizing menu then hold down the letter M and use the down arrow cursor key to bring the window back on to the screen.

12. From the Start menu in Windows click on Settings, Control Panel and then on the Mouse icon. There you will find a range of settings that control the way your mouse behaves. There's also the opportunity to change the button configuration, useful if you are left-handed. The two most important parameters for PC newcomers are Motion and Click Speed; set both to slow and you'll find the mouse much easier to control. Increase the speed once you get used to how the mouse reacts. Whilst you're there click on the Pointers tab and the Scheme menu, then select the Animated Hourglasses option. This will make waiting for things to happen just a little more interesting. . .

13. Here is an easy way to access the contents of your desktop from the Start button, without having to close or minimise any windows. Right-click on the Start button and choose Open, then on the Start Menu window that appears go to the File menu, select New and Shortcut. The Create Shortcut window opens and in the Command Line box type in the following: 'Explorer /root,' ignore the inverted commas but be sure there's a space between Explorer and the forward-slash, and don't forget the comma after root. Click Next and a window opens asking you to 'Select a title for the program'. Back space to delete the default entry and call it 'Desktop' (or anything else you fancy) and click Finish. The item should now appear on the Start menu, if you click it a window containing the contents of your desktop will open. To remove it from the Start menu go Start > Settings > Taskbar & Start Menu > Start Menu Programs tab and click the Remove button. Find the shortcut on the directory and click Remove.

14. Bored with your desktop and all those dull little icons? Then do something about it! You can easily create your own icons in Windows using ordinary picture files or graphics created using the Paint program. You could have the pictures of the family or pets representing your programs (no jokes about using a photo of the mother in law to represent the word processor please. . .), or design your own from scratch. The image can be any size – Windows will automatically adjust the size and shape – but it must be in the Bitmap (extension .bmp) format. Most paint and graphics programs have a 'Save As' facility that will convert picture files from other file types into .bmp format. Once that's done open Windows Explorer, find the picture file and click once into the name field to highlight it, then wait a second and click again to insert a cursor so it can be renamed. Change the file extension from .bmp to .ico, and hit return. Now go to the Desktop and right-click on the icon you want to change and select Properties. On the Shortcut tab you should see a 'Change Icon' button (you can't normally change the icon on Windows applications), click it and use the Browse button to find your icon picture file, press OK and it's done.

15. The double-pane view of Windows Explorer makes it easy to navigate around files and folders; if you like you can force all other Explorer type Folders (My Computer, Control Panel, Recycle Bin, etc.) to open with double panes. Open a folder, My Computer will do, click Folder Options on the View menu and select the File Types tab. Scroll down the list under Registered File Types to find 'Folder', double click on it and in the dialogue window that appears, under Actions, highlight 'Explore', click Set As Default and then Close. To return to the original single pane view, follow the above procedure, but this time select 'Open' in the Actions box.

16. If you've had your PC for more than a year or so the desktop is probably starting to get a bit crowded. Of course you can always remove icons and shortcuts you rarely use but if you're the sort of person who hates to part with anything, here's a simple way of packing even more icons onto your desktop, by reducing the space between them. If you can find an empty area on the desktop click into it and the Display Properties window should appear. Select the Appearance tab and under Item highlight Icon Spacing (horizontal). Change the value from the default setting to 30 and click Apply. Now do the same with Icon Spacing (vertical). You may need to experiment with different values and watch out for large overlapping Icon labels. If that becomes a problem edit the text by clicking slowly into the label box three times or reduce the size of the actual icon – the option is on the same drop down menu as Icon Spacing.

17. This tip will let you start your ten favourite applications with a single key press, and it gives the numeric keypad on the right side of your keyboard something to do. First press the Num Lock key on your keyboard then right-click your mouse on any desktop shortcut and select Properties. Click the cursor into the 'Shortcut Key' field and press the number key on the numeric keypad that you want to start the program with. Click OK and repeat for up to nine other programs. Unless you have a good memory it's a good idea to make a list. If you use the keypad then you can assign some other infrequently used key or key combination, though make sure it's not used by something else . . .

CRASH PROTECTION

18. A common cause of Windows crashes or lock-ups is too many programs running at the same time. You might be lucky and get a warning that something bad is about to happen – a slow running program is a sign of impending danger – but you can keep an eye on what is happening, and possibly prevent a crash, using a simple utility called the Resource Meter. It is quite well hidden. From the Start button select Programs, then Accessories and click on System Tools. Double click on Resource Meter and a small bar-graph icon will appear on the Taskbar, next to the clock. Placing the mouse pointer over the icon will give you an instant readout of the percentage of resources being used, better still click on it and a set of three bar graphs will appear. Problems can occur when any of the three meters falls below 25%. If that happens you should close one or more programs, not forgetting to save any open files first, reboot and all should be well again.

19. Thunderstorms can be fatal for PCs. Strikes on nearby overhead cables and sub-stations can send high voltage 'spikes' down mains supplies, frying computers and other electronic devices. It's sensible to switch your PC off, disconnect the mains plug and telephone modem lead during a thunderstorm, even if it's not directly overhead. If that's not possible then it is worth investing in surge protection devices, for the mains and telephone connections. Protection devices, built into mains sockets or multi-way adaptors are relatively inexpensive – £20 to £50 – compared with the cost of a PC and loss of data. Telephone line protectors start at around £40 and are readily available from PC stockists.

20. Make sure your PC is well ventilated as the combination of a hot office and poor air flow can result in erratic behaviour. Check that the fan is working properly and if there is a build-up of dust around the grille, clear it with a clean paintbrush. Use a vacuum cleaner hose to suck out fluff and debris from the back of the machine. Remove any clutter from the front and side ventilation slots. Don't forget the monitor, now would be a good time to file those papers that are piling up on the top and blocking the vents. Peel off any stickers and furry creatures that could obstruct cooling air.

FASTER WINDOWS

21. If your PC is starting to get a bit sluggish and files seem to take longer to open, you may be able to pep up its performance with a few simple changes. Open the Control Panel and click on the System icon. Select the Performance tab and click on the File System button. On the Hard disk tab you will see a box marked Typical Role of this machine. Change the selection to Network Server. While you're there, make sure the slider marked Read Ahead Optimisation is fully turned up. Click on Apply and re-start your PC.

22. Does your Windows 98 desktop PC seem to be taking longer and longer to boot up? Here's a totally safe way to claw back several valuable seconds, and it's only seven mouse clicks away! Go to the Start menu and proceed thus: Settings > Control Panel > System, select the Performance tab, then the File System button and the Floppy Disk tab and deselect the item 'Search for new floppy disk drives each time your system starts'. The facility is meant for laptop machines, which use detachable external floppy drives. Since the drive on your desktop PC is permanently attached there is no need for Windows to look for a new one; this pointless activity wastes three or four seconds of boot up time on some machines. Don't scoff, three seconds a day, say, 250 days a year comes to twelve and a half minutes a year, in only four and a bit years this simple tweak will have saved you almost one hour – use this time wisely!

23. The following tip may be of interest if you are using a Windows 98 PC with more than 64Mb of RAM. It's all to do with the way Windows manages your PC's RAM and 'virtual' memory, which is space that is set aside on the hard-disk. Anyway, this tip might just make your PC do some things a bit quicker. Open Windows Notepad (Start > Programs > Accessories) and use Open on the File menu to show System.ini, which is in the Windows folder. You may have to change the 'Files of Type' line in the Open dialogue box to 'All Files'. When System.ini appears scroll down the file until you get to the section headed '[386Enh]' and at the end add the following entry: 'ConservativeSwapfileUseage=1' (without the quotes of course), click Save and re-boot. Try it for a few days, you may be pleasantly surprised.

24. If your hard disk is nearly full and you quickly want to free up some space you can quickly claw back at least 4.5 megabytes by deleting unused tutorial animations in Windows Help. Open Windows Explorer, then the Windows folder and double click on Help. Scroll down the list looking for camcorder icons with names like Paste, Scroll, Sizewin, Taskswch and Whatson, they should be listed as Video Clips. Highlight each one in turn and press the delete key (or right-click the mouse button and select delete). Initially they'll be sent to the Recycle Bin, so the space won't become available until the Bin is emptied.

25. If you have just bought a new application or peripheral it is tempting to rip off the packaging and load or install it straight away but before you do, just ask yourself when was it made, and how long has that box been sitting around in warehouses or on dealer's shelves? The chances are whatever it is will be at least several months old and in the time between it being manufactured and you loading it into your PC all sorts of problems may have come to light, and you could end up spending the rest of the holidays trying to get hold of helpline support. Save yourself the inevitable headaches by visiting the manufacturer's website first, and make sure there are no compatibility issues or bugs or updates needed that you should know about. . .

INTERNET AND E-MAIL

26. The right button on your mouse can do some interesting tricks when you're looking at Internet web pages. Click anywhere on the page and you'll see a number of options. The most useful one is to add the address of the current page to your favourite list. If you come across a background design, that you'd like to use as wallpaper on your desktop, right click on the pattern and choose the Set as Wallpaper option. Selecting Copy Background puts the image into the clipboard memory, so you can import it into a graphics program, or it can be filed away, as a .gif or .jpg image, in the file or folder of your choice, using the Save Background As. . . option.

27. If your phone is connected to a digital exchange and you have BT Call Waiting or Call Minder services you may experience problems with Internet connections. Windows 95, 98 and ME can automatically switch the Call Waiting bleeper off before you connect. Open Modems in Control Panel and select the General Tab. Click on Dialling Properties and check the box marked 'To Disable Call Waiting Dial' (or 'How I dial from this Location') and in the adjacent box enter # 43 # (hash 43 hash). You will have to manually switch Call Waiting back on again after you log off by dialling * 43 # (star 43 hash). Call Minder generates a 'stutter' dial tone to let you know you have a message waiting; this does not agree with a lot of modems, so before you go on-line pick up your messages by first dialling 1571.

28. One of the main complaints about the Internet is how long it sometimes takes to access and download pages. There's an easy way to speed things up and that is to just load text. Instead of all the pictures, graphics, advertising banners and sounds you will just see icons. If you want to see or hear an item just right click on the icon and you will get the option to load it. In IE3 go to View on the menu bar then Options > Advanced and uncheck the Show Pictures box. On IE4 the procedure is View > Internet Options > Advanced, scroll down to Multimedia and uncheck the appropriate boxes, in IE5 the same options can be found on the Tools menu. A similar facility in Netscape Navigator 3 is listed under Options, simply remove the tick next to Auto Load Images, on version 4 it's listed under Preferences on the Edit menu, click Advanced and uncheck the Automatically Load Images box.

29. There are probably at least one or two Internet websites that you visit frequently – search engines or a particular home page, etc. Rather than waste time opening your browser, manually selecting the address from the favourites list and making the connection, just create a simple keyboard short cut – it's easy! Pressing the keys will take you straight to your chosen website from within any application.

On the Start menu click Favourites, right-click the site you are interested in then select Properties and the Internet Shortcut tab. In the Shortcut Key box you will see 'None', click in a cursor and type a single letter – choose one that relates to the site you can easily remember, such as 'Y' for Yahoo, etc. – the field will now display the assigned shortcut, i.e. 'Ctrl + Alt + Y'. Click OK and try it out. Internet Explorer opens automatically and takes you straight to the website. (If IE is not your chosen browser you will have to open it and manually add the website address to the Favourites list.)

30. Web pages can often be difficult to read especially if text colours clash with fancy backgrounds and patterns. On Microsoft Internet Explorer there's a very handy feature that will allow you to make quite significant changes to the way web pages are displayed, and in particular the colours used for website addresses that you have and haven't visited and the so-called 'hover' colour. The latter is the colour change that occurs when your mouse pointer passes over and highlights a web address. Open Explorer and on the View menu choose Internet Options, select the General tab and click the Colours button at the bottom of the window. To change a default click on the appropriate colour block and choose a new one from the palette which appears, or create your own custom colour. A similar feature is available on Netscape Navigator on the Options menu under General Preferences.

31. These days creating your own web pages couldn't be simpler and you can let your imagination and artistic inclinations run wild. Unfortunately some web page designers, and that includes professionals who should know better, sometimes make a right hash of it when it comes to displaying text on web pages. Coloured or patterned backgrounds and excessively light or dark text can make reading difficult, impossible in some cases, but here's a quick and easy way to make the words stand out. Just press the Ctrl + Alt keys and all of the text on display will be highlighted, making it much easier to read.

32. Heavy-duty Internet users, here's a way to save yourself several seconds a week by increasing the dialling speed of your PC and modem. It may not work with some modems or phone lines but it's worth a try. Go to Control Panel click on the Modem icon, then Properties and select the Connection tab and click on Advanced. In the Extra Settings field enter S11=50 then click OK. S11 determines the duration of each tone pulse, in milliseconds, the second number specifies the gap between each tone, thus reducing the number to 45 say, makes it dial even faster, increasing the number slows it down. If the connection fails or becomes unreliable simply clear the Extra Settings field to return to the default values.

33. You can check up on your PC's connection speed to the Internet with a few simple clicks. Whilst on-line a small double monitor icon appears in the

System Tray, next to the clock: if you place the mouse pointer over it you will see a summary of bytes sent and received and modem connection speed. Click on the icon and the disconnect dialogue box appears, with the same information displayed. However, unless the modem has been properly configured the connection speed may appear impossibly high, at 115,200 bits/sec. This is the speed at which the PC is communicating with the modem, rather than the speed of data flowing down the telephone line. To remedy that you will need to program the modem with an AT command to display transfer speed in the dialogue box. Open Control Panel and double click on the Modem icon, make sure your modem is highlighted on the General tab, select Properties, then the Connection tab and then the Advanced Button. In the field marked Extra settings enter one of the following commands – if one doesn't work try another. W2 (for modems with Rockwell chipsets), AT&F1 (3COM and USR models) or MR=2 (later Rockwell models and PCI cards). If you still see 115,200 bits/sec try your modem manual or visit the manufacturer's website and look for the Report DCE speed (Data Communication Equipment) command line.

34. One of the most annoying tricks websites pull is to open multiple browser windows, and 'pop-ups' usually without so much as a by your leave. This can happen very quickly and in some cases they open faster than you can close them, or they open in 'Kiosk' mode, where there's no close or minimise icons to click on. The trick is to use the Windows shortcut Ctrl + W to close them quickly, one by one. You could also use the Alt+F4 shortcut, but it's more of a stretch and there's the danger that if you get a bit careless you might shut another program down as well.

35. A lot of people are naturally concerned that private files on their Windows PCs could be opened or 'hacked' whilst they are connected to the Internet. In practice this is extremely unlikely; however, you can reassure yourself and make sure it won't happen by ensuring that no-one has enabled the facility that allows external access to your PC's hard drive. From the Start menu select Settings then Control Panel and double click on the Network icon. Now click on the File and Print Sharing button and make sure that the item 'I want to be able to give others access to my files' is unchecked.

36. It can be incredibly frustrating waiting for Internet pages to appear, especially at peak times, you may even start wondering if you are still connected, or maybe your browser program has frozen. Here's a quick and simple test; whilst on-line with your browser open go to Start > Programs > MSDOS, to open up a DOS window. At the flashing prompt type 'ping' (without the inverted commas) followed by the Internet site address, e.g. ping www.telegraph.co.uk. This will call up the website four times and measure how long it takes to reply, in milliseconds (ms), showing minimum, maximum and average times. Anything under 200 ms is normal, any longer and your connection is slow or the Internet is very busy and you should try again later.

37. Here's a quick one for people who use Outlook Express to collect their e-mail when away from home, on other people's PCs, Internet Café PCs or laptops. By default OE downloads messages from the server to the PC, which can be awkward if it's not your machine. To stop that happening go to Tools and then Accounts, highlight the account you're using and select Properties. Click on the Advanced tab and check the item 'Leave a copy of message on server'. Now you can read your messages when you are away, and when you get home you can download them onto your main PC.

38. Just how secure is your PC? If you want to give yourself a really nasty shock there's an excellent Internet site that automatically tests the integrity of your machine and its defences – or lack of them... With your permission it simulates the kind of surreptitious backdoor snooping an intruder might use to gain access to your system. The utility is called Shields Up! It's free to use and it can be found at: http://grc.com/. If that doesn't convince you of the need for a Firewall on your PC, nothing will!

39. This simple tweak can help reduce the time it takes for your PC to make a connection to your Internet Service Provider, but only try this if it's a stand-alone machine, i.e. not hooked up to a network. Open Dial Up Networking by going to Start > Programs > Accessories > Communications > Dial Up Networking. Right click on the icon for your ISP connection and select Properties and the Server Types tab. In Advanced Options uncheck 'Log on to Networks' and below that, under Allowed Networks make sure that only TCP/IP is checked. Click OK and give it a try, if all's well Internet Explorer (or your chosen browser) should log on and establish a connection a little faster than before. In the unlikely event that anything odd happens simply go back to Dial Up Networking and restore the default settings (i.e. Log on to Networks, NetBeui and IPX/SPX all checked).

40. On Internet Explorer it is possible to open a second smaller browser window by clicking on a link, so you can still see, and quickly return to the original page without reloading it. Just hold down the shift button before left-clicking on the link. Here are some more IE4/5 keyboard shortcuts. Ctrl + D adds the current web page to your Favourite list. Ctrl + H opens the History folder, Ctrl + N opens a new browser window, Ctrl + W closes the active browser window and Ctrl + R reloads the page you are viewing.

41. If you are using Outlook Express and you receive and send a lot of e-mail then your Inbox and Outbox folders could be swallowing up a lot of valuable hard disk space. Get into the habit of regularly 'compacting' the files, this can also make them small enough to backup to a floppy disk. Click and highlight the selected Inbox or Outbox folder icon then go to the File menu, select Folder and Compact Folder.

42. This handy little trick can help make sending e-mails easier. It will put a new icon on your Start menu. When you click on it a blank e-mail message window opens from where you can compose and send an e-mail, without waiting for Outlook Express to open. Move your mouse pointer to the Start button, right-click on it and select Explore from the menu that appears. When the Explorer window opens, right-click in an empty spot in the right-hand pane and select New, then Shortcut. The Create Shortcut dialogue box should appear; under Command Line type in 'mailto:' (leaving off the quotation marks) then click on Next. Now you can give your shortcut a name, clear the highlighted default name and type in something like 'e-mail' or 'messend', and select close. Now go to the Start menu and try out your new high-speed message system.

43. Using the same basic procedure you can create a personalised message window for anyone that you frequently send e-mails to, with their address automatically inserted. As before, right-click into an empty part of the desktop, select New and then Shortcut from the menu. In the window that appears, in the Command Line field, type:

mailto:friendsname@freebienet.com

where the part after mailto: is the recipient's e-mail address. Click Next, give your new Shortcut a name then click Finish.

44. Here's a way to turn your Internet Explorer/Outlook Express e-mail Address Book into a text file that can be read by a word processor, or imported into other e-mail programs. Open Address Book and on the File menu select Export, then **Address Book**. In the dialogue box that appears select 'Text File (comma separated values)' and click the Export button. Type in the path (where you want the file to be stored) and give the file a name, for example: C:\my documents\adbook.txt. Select Next, check the items you wish to export and click Finish.

45. Did you know that in Outlook Express 5 you can attach a sound file to an e-mail that will play automatically as soon as it is opened on the recipient's computer? You can specify how many times it's played, or even make it play continuously, if you really want to annoy someone, the possibilities – for good and mischief – are endless. . .
   First record your sound as a *.wav file using Windows Sound Recorder (Start > Programs > Accessories > Entertainment) most PCs these days have a microphone input. Create your message as usual in the New Message window, on the Format menu make sure Rich Text (HTML) is checked, click anywhere in the message window and go to Background on the Format menu, select Sound and use the Browse button to locate your sound file, set the number of plays, click OK and send your message.

46. If you receive a lot of messages on the same topic, or from the same sender (maybe you print out a lot of e-mails) then there is a very convenient but little known feature in Outlook Express that allows you to combine messages into one document, for reading or printing. Open the mailbox containing the messages you want to combine and highlight them by hold down the Ctrl key and clicking on each one in turn. Now go to the Messsage menu and select Combine and Decode. You will be asked if you want to change the order of the messages, if not click OK and the new combined document will be created, use SaveAs on the file menu to save it as a new document.

47. Here is a way to send a photograph with an e-mail, by inserting it into the actual message. This only works when your e-mail client program –

we'll assume you are using Outlook or Outlook Express – is set to send HTML (Hypertext mark-up language) and the person you are sending it to can receive HTML messages. Click on the New Message icon, go to the Format drop-down menu and make sure 'Rich Text (HTML)' is selected. Now all you have to do is compose your message as normal and when you come to the point where you want the picture to go click on the Insert Picture icon (it looks like a postcard) then use the Browse button to locate the image file. It will appear in the message window, as the recipient will see it. Finish your message and send it as normal.

48. If you are using Internet Explorer V5 and you haven't tried Internet radio yet, there's a radio tuner facility hidden away inside your browser. To enable it click on Tools > Internet Options and select the Advanced tab. Scroll down the list to the Multimedia heading and check the item 'Always Show Internet Explorer Radio Bar'. Click okay and exit the dialogue box. Now right-click into an empty area of the toolbar and select Radio from the drop-down menu. A new toolbar appears, click on Radio Stations and Radio Station Guide, which will take you to the Windows Media radio tuner home page. From there you can select a list of stations according to style, content, language, etc. This will either take you to the station's home page, and a live 'listen' button, which lets you hear what's going on through Windows Media Player. (Be patient, it can take a few seconds before you hear anything, as the data has to be 'buffered' in the PC's memory to prevent breaks in sound caused by heavy traffic on the Internet.) Some stations may require you to have special player software but there is usually a link on the page to the appropriate download website.

49. Some modems just won't play ball and stubbornly refuse to work with Windows or do strange things, like randomly dropping the line, or operating at ridiculously low data rates. If yours is playing up it's worth trying a standard Windows modem driver. Open Control Panel and click on Add/Remove Hardware, click Next until you get to the screen that asks you if you want Windows to look for new devices, select No, on the 'Hardware Types' list double-click the Modem icon, check 'Don't detect my modem...' and click Next. Make sure 'Standard Modem Types' is highlighted under 'Manufacturers'. In the right pane select 'Standard 56000bps V90' or the option that best matches your modem, click Next and continue to the end. To revert to your previous custom driver remove the Standard Modem entry in Device Manager (right-click My Computer and select Properties), re-boot and Windows will detect your modem and re-install the original driver (have your driver disk to hand).

FATTER FASTER FILES

50. Every so often you may want to transfer files between PCs on floppy disk. It's no problem, providing the file is no larger than 1.4Mb. If it is you could compress the data, or use multiple floppies, but there's another option, compress the disk. Windows 95 (and 98) has a utility called DriveSpace. It is intended to increase the capacity of hard disk drives, but it works just as well with floppies, almost doubling their capacity, to around 2.6Mb. Insert a clean disk into drive A: and from the Start Menu click on Programs, then Accessories then System Tools and open DriveSpace. Click on the disk icon or choose compress from the File menu and follow the instructions.

51. If you need to make a copy of a floppy disk quickly – maybe a colleague needs to see some files you've been working on – then Windows can help. From your desktop or the Start Button open My Computer then right-click on the floppy disk icon and select Copy Disk on the menu. Windows then reads the entire contents of the disk into the PC's memory; a bar graph shows how the copy process is progressing. When the indicator reaches halfway Copy Disk will ask you to remove the original disk and load a blank formatted floppy. Make sure there's nothing on it or it may be overwritten, click OK and the information is read back to the second disk.

52. Send To is one of the most useful facilities in Windows Explorer. By right clicking on a file, the Send To option will instantly copy the file to another folder, a floppy disk or the clipboard, but it can do many more things besides. You can add any application or drive destination to the Send To list and save yourself a lot of time moving files and opening applications.

Go to the Start menu then Programs and open Windows Explorer. Scroll down the list to the Windows folder, open it, locate and double click on Send To. Now go up to File on the menu bar, select New, then Shortcut and use Browse to find the application you are interested in. Open the folder and look for the relevant *.exe file, single click to highlight and select Open. You will be asked to give the program a name – if you don't want to use the default – then click Next and Finish and the item is added to the Send To list.

PRINTER PROBLEMS

53. Having problems with your printer? You may be surprised to know Windows 95 comes with a sophisticated printer troubleshooting program. It's on the CD-ROM, you can find it with Windows Explorer, click on the D: drive icon, then open the Other folder and inside you'll find a folder called Misc, open that and then the Epts (enhanced printer troubleshooter). Click on epts.exe and the program starts, first analysing your printer set-up, it then asks a series of questions and suggests remedies to help you solve the problem. The troubleshooter is built into Windows 98, just open Windows Help and type Troubleshooting into the Index Windows and select Printers from the list.

54. If you have a paper jam do not force it. Always try to remove the blockage in the normal direction of travel, if it tears make sure all of the fragments are removed. If you can't clear the paper path refer to the manual. Store paper flat in the original packaging, always fan it before loading to free up the sheets and stop them sticking together. If the paper hopper is partially full always load it so the old paper is used first. Always check to make sure the paper you are using is within the printer's handling limits. Keep printers well away from radiators and out of strong sunlight – especially laser printers – as this can affect print quality.

55. If you regularly need to switch between two settings on your printer (i.e. portrait and landscape mode, etc.) when printing from different applications, you can avoid a lot of messing around by making Windows believe you have two or more printers. Open the Printers folder in My Computer and click on Add New Printer and follow through the installation procedure for your existing printer. At the point when Windows asks the printer's name change to default, Printer 2 for example. When the setup is complete right-click on the new printer icon, select Properties and change the settings as required. Now all you have to do is select the new printer in your application's Printer Setup dialogue box, or simply drag and drop the file onto the Printer 2 icon.

56. Here's a way to squeeze a little extra speed out of most printers. By default Windows is set to spool print jobs. That basically means the data to be printed is first written to a temporary file, which allows you and the PC to get on with other jobs, whilst the printer is working. If you turn off the

Print Spooler you should find print jobs take less time to complete. The option can be found by right-clicking your printer icon from the Printers Folder in My Computer or Start > Settings. Select Properties, then the Details tab and click on the Spool Settings button. Click 'Print Directly To Printer' then OK. The only disadvantage is that on long print jobs you may see the busy icon in your application more often than usual. Be warned that it doesn't work on all systems and all printers so try it on a test document first – time a print job before and after switching off the spooler – if you encounter problems click the Restore Defaults button in the print spooler dialogue window.

COMFORT AND SAFETY

57. Computers can seriously damage your health! Inappropriate seating is a major contributing factor to back pain. If you are going to be seated in front of your PC for more than an hour or so each day get a proper chair. Purpose designed office chairs, with adjustable height and back support are ideal, and they're not expensive.

58. Make sure your display screen is at the most comfortable height – e.g. eye-level – and that the brightness and contrast are properly adjusted. If you get a lot of reflections on the screen, from bright lights or windows, a clip-on anti-glare screen should help. Don't sit staring at the screen for hours on end without a break. Stand up from time to time, walk around, maybe do some stretching exercises.

59. Keyboards can cause a lot of problems, especially the cheap ones that come with a lot of PCs these days. Fast typists and those used to mechanical typewriters can find the short, sharp keystrokes of a PC keyboard uncomfortable, it can even lead to painful repetitive strain injury or RSI. If you're going to be doing a lot of typing think about buying an ergonomically shaped keyboard. Wrist support pads can help relieve the strain, though if problems persist you should consult your GP.

60. If you have poor or failing eyesight computer display screens can be difficult to read. If you find the icons and printing underneath too small to read easily try the 'large' and 'extra large' colour Schemes in Display Properties. They're located on the Appearances Tab that you can find by double clicking on the Display icon in Control Panel. While you are there select the Settings tab and try the 'Larger Fonts' size. You may also find it helpful to change the Desktop Area slider to a lower value, especially if it has been set to a high resolution figure (1024 x 768 pixels, for example) and you are viewing it on a 14- or 15-inch monitor. Most word-processor packages have a 'zoom' facility, to enlarge the size of the text display.

A similar set of options is available from the Accessibility Options icon in Control Panel. Double click the icon to open the window. Select the Display tab, then Settings. The next set of options will enlarge the display, with normal black on white text, or the whole thing can be reversed, with white on black characters. Click on display, then check the Use High Contrast box and confirm the changes by clicking the Apply button. Be patient, it takes a few seconds for the display to change.

61. You can easily change the font and size of the typeface used by Windows Explorer and icon labelling. It's worth trying if you find it difficult to read, you're using an unusually large or small monitor, or you're simply bored with the default typeface. Right click your mouse on an empty space on the desktop and select Properties, when the Display window appears click on the Appearance tab. In the drop-down menu marked Item, choose Icon. You will then be able to select a new typeface from the Font menu.

HIDDEN UTILITIES

62. System Monitor allows you to visually check the data throughput of an external modem, in real time. It can be found by clicking the Start button, then Accessories and System Tools. Open System Monitor and click on the Edit menu then Add Item. Select Dial Up Adapter from the list in the Category Window and Bytes Received/Second and Bytes Transmitted/Second in the Item Window, then OK. (Note, System Monitor is not installed by default so you may have to load it from your Windows CD-ROM using Add/Remove Programs in Control Panel.)

63. How well do you know your Windows 98 PC? Tucked away inside your machine is a complete history of its inner workings, charting system settings and changes to the hardware and software configuration. It's useful to have a permanent record of this information made when your PC is working normally. There are some interesting facts and figures in amongst the mass of gobbledegook and if at some stage something goes wrong, it could help you or a PC savvy friend to track down the problem more easily. To produce such a file go to Start > Programs > Accessories > System Tools > System Information. On the File menu select Export, give the file a name – something along the lines 'mypc.txt' – choose a location and click Save. You could print it out but be warned that it can run to more than 100 pages!

64. If you keep a lot of images on your Windows 95/98 PC it can very useful to see what is stored in folders, without opening a paint program and sifting through the files manually. Windows Explorer has a well-hidden utility for generating thumbnail views of picture files. It is disabled by default, probably because it slows Explorer down, but you can enable it selectively, so it only works on folders containing image files. Here's what you do: open Windows Explorer and right-click on the folder you wish to view. From the drop-down menu that appears select Properties and the General tab. Check the item 'Enable thumbnail view' and click Apply, then OK. Go to the View menu and click Refresh, and a new item 'Thumbnails' should appear above Large Icons on both the View menu and the drop down menu next to the Views icon on the Toolbar. Select it and the display will change to a screen full of mini preview pictures.

65. Hardware Info carries out a comprehensive check on driver files and the hardware attached to the machine, flagging up potential problems with colour-coded highlights. Error information is displayed in red, and warnings in blue. To start Hardware Info go to Run on the Start menu and type 'hwinfo /ui' (omitting the inverted commas of course) and then click OK. It only takes a few seconds after which the report appears. Check through the report looking for any red or blue highlights, which may indicate trouble, or potential trouble, and require further investigation. If you know a thing or two about PCs you may want to have a look at the alternative reports on the View menu. If your PC and hardware is behaving normally it's probably be a good idea to leave well alone, but take note of any warnings and save your Hwinfo file for future reference or to show to an engineer.

66. The Version Conflict Manager Utility or VCMUI should be of interest to anyone who routinely updates their software applications. This can cause problems when files from older or newer versions of a program conflict with one another. If you've had difficulty with a recent update VCMUI should track down the offending files, and might even provide a solution, it can also highlight potential conflicts before they've had a chance to cause problems. To give your PC's software a quick health check go to Run on the Start menu and type 'VCMUI', without the quotes of course. All being well you'll see an empty dialogue box, indicating that your applications are conflict-free; if not just follow the instructions.

67. System File Checker can help engineers and knowledgeable users to track down and automatically correct common problems. It's worth running the SFC every now and again, especially on well-used machines, and you never know, it may help to resolve a long-running problem; however, unless you know what you are doing it is a good idea to leave the settings on their defaults. To start the program go to Run on the Start menu and type 'sfc.exe' and click Start to begin the checking routine.

68. CheckLinks can be found on the Windows 98 CD-ROM and its job is to weed out shortcuts and Start menu items that no longer do anything. It's not going to save you much disk space but 'broken links' can sometimes cause problems and point to programs that you no longer need or use. The Link Check Wizard can be found by going to the Tools folder, then Reskit and Desktop, click on the chklnks.exe icon and follow the instructions. If you like you can copy and paste chklnk.exe to your hard drive, and include it with your regular hard disk maintenance routines.

69. How many applications are running on your PC right now? It's easy to lose track, and if your system's resources fall to dangerously low levels Windows will crash, often without warning. Windows 9x and ME have a built-in monitoring utility but it's not enabled by default; there are two ways to get to it, via Start > Programs > Accessories > System Tools, or simply type 'RSRCMTR' into Run on the Start menu. This will put a little bar graph into the System Tray (next to the clock). If it shows two or more green bars you should be okay – double click the icon for more detailed information. It's well worth having this on display all of the time; to do this open the Start-up folder (Start > Programs) then go to Start > Programs > Accessories > System Tools, hold down the Ctrl key and drag the Resource meter icon into the Start-up folder and it will open automatically every time your PC boots up. If by any chance you can't see Resource Meter in System Tools go to Add/Remove Programs in Control Panel and select the Windows Setup tab, double-click System Tools, check the item System Resource Meter, click OK and follow the on-screen prompts.

SCREEN GEMS

70. If you want to launch a screen-saver quickly – maybe you're going out to lunch or prevent others from seeing what's on your screen – open Windows Explorer, go to the Windows folder and open the System file. There you will find all of the Windows screen-saver files. They're easy to spot as they have monitor-shaped icons and end with the file extension *.scr. Right click on the icon, select 'Send To' then 'Desktop as Shortcut', when you want to start it in a hurry just double-click on the desktop icon.

71. Display Properties is one of the most frequently used items in Control Panel, so why is it so difficult to get at? Here's a way to open it with a single click from your desktop or Quick Launch toolbar, and you can even specify which tab it opens on, so you could go directly to the Settings or Screensaver page. Here's how. Right-click on the desktop and select New then Shortcut. In the Command Line type in 'control desk.cpl' (without the quotes), click Next and give it a name. To make it open on a particular tab add two commas and then a number from 0 to 5 (i.e. 'control desk.cpl,,1' for the Screensaver tab, 'control desk.cpl,,3 for Settings, etc.). You can leave the shortcut where it is on the desktop or drag it into the Quick Launch toolbar. If you want to change the opening tab just right-click on the shortcut and select Properties and change the command in the 'Target' line.

72. If you're bored with the standard Windows 98 and ME colours for title bars on windows and message boxes here's a quick way to cheer them up with a very snazzy 'gradient' colour, which changes gradually from one colour to another. This trick works best if your PC is set to True Colour or High Colour, to check right-click onto an empty part of the desktop, select Properties from the menu and click the Settings tab. To create your colour gradient stay with Display Properties and select the Appearance tab. Click on the Active Window title bar in the display window then click on Colour, a palette of 12 colours appears with the facility to create a colour of your choice by selecting the 'Other' button. Now click on Colour 2 and select a second colour, the effect is immediately displayed. Have fun, experiment with some bright and outrageous shades; it can really brighten up your desktop!

73. Newcomers to Windows often find the scroll bars at the side and bottom of word processor and spreadsheet screens quite difficult to use. The bars are narrow and the slider can be hard to control, until you get used to it. It's easy to change the size of the bars; even seasoned users may prefer to make them a little wider. To make the change go to Control Panel, click on the Display icon and select the Appearance tab. Click in the middle of the scroll bar shown in the 'Active Window', in the display. The word 'Scrollbar' should appear in the box below marked Item, along with a pair of up/down arrows and the default setting of 16. Try 20 or 25 but if you want to see something really funny whizz it up to the maximum of 100!

74. If you're spending several hours each day staring at your computer's monitor screen it's important to make sure it is properly set-up. Incorrect picture settings can result in fatigue, headaches and eyestrain. Adjusting brightness and contrast by eye can be quite difficult. Monitors also go out of alignment, but some picture faults – such as slowly deteriorating focus, geometry or colour registration – are difficult to spot in their early stages. For that reason it's worth periodically checking your monitor with a program such as Ntest. It was created by Nokia's monitor division and features a dozen test patterns, to help you set up your monitor and give it a complete health check. What's more it's free! You can download the self-extracting Ntest program from:

   http://www.listsoft.com/progs/pr3071.htm

75. Create your own personal screensaver. If you have the OSR2 release of Windows 95 or Windows 98/ME click on the Start button go to Settings, then Control Panel and double-click on the Display icon. Select the Screensaver tab and scroll down the list until you come to '3D Text'. Highlight the entry and click on the Settings button. You can enter your name or a message – up to 16 characters and spaces long – in the text field, that will bounce or wobble around the screen, or you can choose an animated digital clock display. Click on the Texture buttons and try some of the *.bmp files in the Windows folder. This screensaver also contains an 'Easter egg' a hidden novelty feature planted by the programmers. Type the word 'Volcano' into the text field, click OK and see what happens. . .

76. A pound to a penny says your Windows 95/98 Taskbar is still in its default position at the bottom of the screen, taking up valuable screen space. Maybe you've enabled the Hide Taskbar facility (Start > Settings Taskbar &

Start menu) so it doesn't take up any room when you are working, but it still pops into view every so often, when your mouse strays close to the bottom of the screen. So why not move it? The most logical place has to be the right or left side of your screen. The right-hand side in particular is often a 'dead' area in programs like word processors and since a VDU screen is over 30% wider than it is tall; you can afford to lose a little room at the side. To move the Taskbar simply put the mouse pointer into an empty area of the Taskbar, right-click and hold and drag it to its new location. You can enable Auto Hide, or better still, leave it on show and more accessible, then re-size your application to fit, so that it doesn't obscure scroll bars; most Windows programs will 'remember' a new layout whenever they are opened.

SOUNDS INTERESTING

77. If you're bored with the cheesy tunes, 'pings' and 'ta-da' Windows sounds, create your own from snippets of audio CDs, played in the CD-ROM drive. Load the CD and open the Sound Recorder by clicking on Start then Programs, Accessories and Multimedia (or Entertainment in Windows 98). Play the CD (the Audio CD player is also in Accessories > Multimedia/Entertainment) and click on the Sound Recorder red record button. You may need to adjust the level or enable the input from the CD player from Volume Control on the View menu on CD Player. Sound Recorder can also add special effects (echo, play backwards, change speed) and edit the sound (Delete Before/After on the edit menu). When you are happy with it, give it a name and save it in the Media folder in Windows. It can then be accessed easily from the Sounds utility in Control Panel and assigned to an event of your choice. Remember, no public performances if you're recording Copyright material!

78. Why not create your own sounds? All you need is a microphone; plug it into the 'mic' jack socket on the PC's sound card or audio input. It should be on the back of your PC, close to the speaker plug. Find the sound recorder utility, it's in the Multimedia folder in the Accessories directory. It's easy to use, just like an ordinary tape recorder; full instructions are in the associated help file. When you've recorded your sound give it a name. From the File menu choose 'Save As' and put it in the Media directory in the Windows folder, then go back to the Sounds icon in Control Panel and assign it to the event of your choice.

79. You will often find that you want to change the volume of your PC's sound system; however, the volume control is not very accessible on a standard Windows installation. Normally most users get to it via the View menu option in CD Player (Start > Programs > Accessories > Multimedia > CD Player > View > Volume Control) but there's a quicker way, and you can have it permanently on the taskbar if you so wish. From the Start menu click on Settings, then Control Panel and the Multimedia icon. Click on it and select the Audio tab. About halfway down there's a small box marked Show Volume Control on the Taskbar. Check the box and it's done. On the far left side of the taskbar you will see a small loudspeaker symbol; when you click on it a volume slider and mute switch will appear on the screen.

80. If you're in the habit of playing audio CDs on your PC it's a good idea to put the CD Player on the Start menu. From the Start menu click on Settings then Taskbar and select the Start Menu Programs tab. Click on the Add then Browse buttons and look for the Windows folder. Double click on it to open it up then move the horizontal slider along until the CD Player icon appears. Highlight it, click open, then next and select the Start Menu folder at the top of the file tree. To complete click next and then Finish.

81. Your multimedia PC has a sound system that is capable of hi-fi performance but you're never going to realise anything like the full sonic potential of audio CDs and games with those speakers. . . The speakers supplied with most PCs have the acoustic properties of baked bean tins. If you've got a redundant hi-fi system or some half-decent speakers lying around, try connecting it to your PC and hear the difference! The soundcards used on most PCs have an amplified output and can drive speakers directly. Suitable leads are available from electrical accessory dealers. Make sure the speakers are at least a foot away from the monitor screen, otherwise the speaker magnets may cause colour staining on the display.

82. Windows 98 and ME has a little known speaker configuration utility that allows you to tailor the sound of your PC according to the size and type of speakers. Go to Start > Settings > Control Panel and select Multimedia, make sure the Audio tab is selected and click the Advanced Properties button. On the Speakers page Desktop Stereo Speakers will probably be selected, but it's surprising how many laptops have that setting too. Try some of the other options – you may have to reboot for any changes to take effect – and the differences can be quite small but it's well worth trying. Whilst you are at it you may want to look at the Performance tab and if your PC is a relatively speedy model with a plenty of RAM, move the two sliders to the maximum setting.

83. To play .wav sounds and music through your PC's or laptop's built-in loudspeaker you will need a little piece of freebie software from Microsoft called Speak.exe. There's a chance it is already on your PC: use the Find utility on the Start menu to check, otherwise you can download it from one of scores of Internet websites, or direct from Microsoft's own file library:

http://support.microsoft.com/download/support/mslfiles/Speak.exe

Next, go to Add New Hardware in Control panel, double click Add, then Next, followed by No, then Next and in the Hardware Types box select Sound Video & Game Controller. Click Next again and Have Disk. Use Browse to find your copy of Speak.exe and click OK. Select Sound Driver for PC Speaker and click OK, then Finish and when prompted re-start the PC. You will find the controls for the PC speaker in Multimedia on the Control Panel; on the Devices tab click the Audio Devices branch and Audio for Sound Driver for PC speaker and then Settings. On Windows 98 you'll find it on the Advanced tab.

WORD PROCESSING

84. The bright white text area of most word processors can become quite tiring on the eyes after a few hours. You can of course jiggle the brightness and contrast settings on your monitor but a far better solution is to give your blank pages a light grey tint. Open your word processor and load a page of text, so you can judge the effect. Next, from the Start button select Settings, Control Panel and the Display icon. Select the Appearance tab and click into the area marked Window Text. Next click on the Color box and choose the Other option. This will bring up a colour palette, select grey or white from the block of colour options and use the slider to the right of the multi-colour panel to adjust the level. Click OK and if necessary re-adjust until you are satisfied with it. The tint only applies to the display and will not affect the way documents look when they are printed.

85. If you are constantly fussing over fonts for your documents then there's a very handy feature in Windows that allows you to quickly compare typefaces according to style and design. From the Start menu go to Settings, then Control Panel and double click the Fonts icon. Go to the View drop-down menu and click on 'List Fonts by Similarity'. Now all you have to do is click on the drop down 'List Fonts. . .', choose a font and you will be presented with list of comparable typefaces, ranked according to similarity.

86. Generally speaking Microsoft Word is fairly reliable, but when it does go wrong it does so in spectacular fashion and in addition to closing itself down without warning, it can also take Windows with it. Word users plagued by persistent problems usually give up and reinstall the program, only to find that nothing has changed. In those circumstances there's almost always a glitch in a file called 'Normal.dot' which contains all of the user's settings, which includes macros and other mischief-makers. If you are about to reinstall Word for the tenth time, try this. Make a copy of your Normal.dot file (just in case it's not corrupt) and save it in another folder, it can usually be found in Windows\Application Data\Microsoft\ Templates, delete the original Normal.dot and re-boot. Word will automatically create a new Normal.dot and return to its default settings.

87. Word users usually manage to find Word Count in the Tools menu; it may be more versatile than you think. As it stands it will count all of the words in an open document, but if you want to know how many words there are in a paragraph, or block of copy, just use the highlight function, then click on word count. You can create a simple keyboard shortcut to Word Count by going to the Tools menu and click on Customise. Select the Command tab; highlight Tools in the list of Categories and scroll down the list of Commands until you come to Word Count. Highlight it, then click on the Keyboard button, put the pointer into the Press New Shortcut field and press the mouse button. Decide which keys you are going to use (Ctrl and backslash '\' are usually free), finish off by clicking Assign and Close.

88. If you habitually work with a lot of open documents in Word you will know how time consuming it can be to save and close each document separately, when you exit the program. There's a hidden set of commands that will speed things up considerably. All you have to do is hold down the shift key and then move the mouse pointer to the File drop-down menu. You will see that Close has changed to Close All, and Save is now Save All. To exit Word in double quick time click Save All, followed by Close All and watch those documents disappear! Incidentally, Word will prompt you to name any untitled documents, so there's no fear of losing track of anything.

89. In Word there's a useful unpublished facility called Random Word. Every so often you might want to create a block of text quickly, to test out your faxing or E-mail facilities, or produce dummy text to check a page layout. You can of course copy and paste text from another document but Random Word is far quicker. Simply type in the following: =rand() and press Return. Word will then generate three paragraphs, each containing the sentence 'The quick brown fox jumps over the lazy dog', five times. You can alter the number of paragraphs and sentences by inserting numbers into the brackets. For example, =rand(6,8) generates a text block of 6 paragraphs, each containing 8 sentences.

90. If you frequently need to insert a word, line or block of text into MS Word documents you can easily automate the process with a simple keyboard shortcut. Highlight the text and press Alt + F3, to create an AutoText entry, then give it a name or accept the default that appears in the dialogue box that appears and click OK. Now go to the Tools menu; select Customise and the Commands Tab. Click the Keyboard button then AutoText in the Categories window. Highlight your new entry in the Commands Window, click a cursor in the Press New Shortcut Key field, choose a key combination then click Assign. To remove an AutoText entry go to the Insert menu, click AutoText, then AutoText, select the AutoText tab, highlight the entry and click Delete.

91. There's a hidden feature in Word 97 & 2000 that automatically scrolls the page or document you're watching. It's really handy for reading long documents, or you can use it to turn your PC screen into a teleprompter or autocue, for displaying speeches and scripts. It was originally designed to be used with 'wheel' type mice but it works on any standard two or three button mouse. Click on Customise on the Tools menu, select the Commands tab, scroll down the list and highlight 'All Commands' in the Categories window. In the right hand Commands window find, single click and hold on Auto Scroll, drag and drop it onto a toolbar and a button will appear. Close Customise and click on the Auto Scroll button, you can vary the speed and direction using the arrows that appears in the left-hand scroll bar.

92. As you may have discovered there is no master list of keyboard shortcuts in Word Help and tracking down a specific command – there are more than 200 of them – or finding out if a particular one even exists, can be a frustrating and time-consuming business. Wonder no more, here's an easy way to print out a complete list of Word shortcuts and commands, to keep by your PC for quick reference.

Go to the Tools menu and click on Macro then Macros. In the 'Macros In' drop-down menu select Word Commands, now move your mouse pointer to the Macro Name pane and highlight ListCommands, click Run and in the dialogue box that appears select Current Menu and Keyboard Settings and click OK. A new document will open, with a table showing all of the available commands and shortcuts. Just use Save As to give it a name and print it out. Be warned in its raw form it runs to around 9 pages (12pt text) but with a little judicious editing of the commands you'll never need or use it can be trimmed to a more manageable 5 to 6 pages.

93. As you know you can insert pictures and graphics into Microsoft Word documents, but did you also know you can add sounds? Try it, it's fun! It works on most recent versions of Word (97 & 2000). Before you start select, create or record the sound you want to use with Windows Sound Recorder (Start > Programs > Accessories > Entertainment) or your preferred audio editing program and save it as a *.wav file. Open Word and position the cursor in the document where you want the sound to be then go to the Insert menu and select Object. Make sure the Create New tab is displayed then scroll down the list to Wave Sound and click on it. Press Okay and a speaker icon appears on the page and Windows Media Player opens. Go to Insert File on the Edit menu, select your audio file and it's done. When anyone double clicks on the speaker icon the sound file will be played.

94. Here's an easy way to find out what the Function keys along the top of the keyboard do in Word 2000. Right-click into an empty area next to the Toolbar at the top of the screen, and select Customise from the drop-down menu. Put a check mark next to 'Function Key display' and a new toolbar will appear at the bottom of the screen, with clickable buttons showing what each key does, plus their alternative functions, when you press the Alt, Shift or Ctrl keys.

95. This very handy little utility will appeal to all users of Office 2000 or any of its components, including Word, Excel, Outlook, and PowerPoint, etc. It's called WOPR 2000 Place Bar Customiser and it's all yours for the price of a two-minute download from the Microsoft website.

WOPR 2000 allows you to modify the Places Bar, that's the row of five folders that appears on the left side of Open and Save As, etc., dialogue boxes used by all Office 2000 applications. The five folders that appear (History, Personal, Favourites, Desktop and Web Folders) cannot normally be changed but with WOPR 2000 you can specify the folders or disk drive that you use most often, making the Place Bar a lot more useful. You can also double the number of folders displayed to ten by selecting the Show Small Icon option. The download file is small – just 423 kilobytes – and is easy to install and configure from a new item that appears on the application's Tools menu. Full details and a link to the download can be found at:

http://officeupdate.microsoft.com/2000/downloadDetails/PlaceBar.htm

JUST FOR FUN

96. The Solitaire game in Windows must be one of the greatest time-wasters of all time – it drives office managers crazy – but even though it is so simple it can be highly addictive. If you're one of the millions hooked on it then you have probably figured out by now that the Draw 3 option – selected by default – slows the game down, increases the odds against you winning and makes it harder to play. Of course you could just switch to easy-peasy Draw 1 setting and play it that way, but where's the fun in that? The next time you're in a fix try this simple little cheat. Press and hold down the Crtl, Alt and Shift keys, then click on the top card and you'll find that you can now select cards one at a time.

We know that the FreeCell and Minesweeper games included in almost all versions of Windows have a devoted following and some may consider what follows as heresy so if you're a purist avert your eyes now because we are about to reveal some simple cheats and enhancements.

In FreeCell you can win instantly by holding down Ctrl + Shift + F10, choose Abort from the menu that appears and drag any card to the top.

To switch off the Minesweeper timer, position the mouse pointer on any grey part of the game window, press and hold the right and left mouse keys and press the Escape key.

Finally, you can add some simple sound effects to Minesweeper by opening Windows Notepad (Start > Programs > Accessories) select All Files then open the 'Winmine.ini' file in the Windows folder (you might want to make a backup copy, just in case). Add the line 'Sound=3' to the end, Save and exit Notepad. If you add a subsequent line 'Tick=1', you'll hear a bleep as the timer counts up.

97. 'Easter Eggs' are diverting little features hidden away inside software applications, and another reason why programs take up so much hard disk space these days... This one is in both Windows 95 and 98. Open Display Properties in Control Panel, select the Screensaver tab, choose 3D Pipes, click the Settings button and check 'Multiple', 'Traditional' and 'Solid'. In Joint Type select Mixed, click OK then Preview and look out for Teapots... No prizes, but can anyone tell us what's so special about this particular teapot?

98. This next one can be found in Windows 98 and is quite challenging, calling for a very steady hand, and possibly an atlas. Double click on the time display on the Taskbar or click on Regional settings in Control Panel and select the Time Zone tab to display the world map. Hold down the Ctrl key and move the mouse pointer to Cairo, at the northern end of the Red Sea, click and hold the left mouse button then move the mouse pointer to Memphis Tennessee (above Florida) release the mouse button, then without moving the pointer click and hold and move the pointer to Redmond in Washington State (just North of San Francisco) release the mouse button, watch, listen and be amazed (well, mildly surprised...). Don't give up if it doesn't work first time, you have to be very precise.

99. This Easter Egg is quite diverting and it lives in Excel 2000. It's a challenging driving game with excellent graphics; note that you will also need DirectX 6 or 7 on your PC, if not you'll find it on most PC magazine cover-mount CD-ROMs.

Pay attention, it's quite involved, but well worth the effort. Open Excel 2000, on the File menu select 'Save As Web Page' then check the items 'Save Selection Sheet' and 'Add Interactivity', click Save and a file called 'page.htm' should end up in My Documents (or wherever else you choose to put it). Exit Excel and open Internet Explorer and open the saved 'page.htm' file. Scroll all the way down to row 2000 and along to column WC, check the cell, highlight the whole line and use tab to select cell 2000 WC again. Next, hold down Ctrl + Shift + Alt and click on the Excel logo in the top left hand corner. The screen goes black and after a few seconds the game starts. Use the arrow keys to steer, the spacebar to fire your guns, H for headlights, O to spray oil and Esc to exit. Good luck!

100. Internet Explorer 5 has its own Easter Egg. On the Tools menu select Internet Options then the General tab and click the Languages button. Select Add and in the User Defined field type 'ie-ee' (minus the quote marks) then click OK. Highlight the entry and click the Move Up button to put it at the top of the list. Select OK to close the windows click on the Search icon and in the side menu you see a new set of options. Select Previous Searches and follow the links on to the Internet to see the guilty ones!

Glossary

8mm

Video and data recording system using 8mm wide magnetic tape; cassettes are roughly the size of an audio cassette.

286, 386, 486

Families of Intel microprocessor chips developed during the 1980s and early 1990s, forerunners of the Pentium chips used in the latest PCs.

ACTIVE-X

Powerful programming tools used to add multimedia components and features to Internet web pages.

ADMIN TEMPLATES

Poledit options that cover a range of Windows features, including how it looks and works, restrictions on Internet and e-mail access, network configuration, etc.

ADSL

Asymmetric Digital Subscriber Line – high speed digital connection using existing telephone lines. ADSL has the facility to be 'always on', so there is no need to dial up a connection.

ASCII

American Standard Code for Information Interchange – a universal data code for text and alphanumeric characters, understood by virtually all computers.

AT

ATtention – the prefix to a modem command, to tell the modem to expect an instruction.

ATAPI

AT Attachment Packet Interface – industry standard disk drive connection system and data communications protocols, used on most CD-rewriters, suitable for use with most Windows PCs.

ATRAC

Adaptive Transform Acoustic Coding – digital audio compression system used by the MiniDisc format.

AUTOCORRECT

Word feature that automatically corrects spelling mistakes as you type.

AUTOTEXT

A frequently used block of text – an address, salutation, etc. – that can be inserted into a document.

AVERY LABELS

A range of standardised label styles and formats, developed by the office equipment company of the same name.

BAD SECTORS

Parts of the hard disk drive which the test utility Scandisk marks as being faulty and incapable of reliably storing data. A sudden increase in the number of bad sectors is often a sign that the drive is damaged or starting to deteriorate.

BCC

Blind Carbon Copy, sends a copy of a message to several recipients, but without showing details of the other recipients on the e-mail.

BETA

Beta software is usually a near final version of a program or application, made available to testers and volunteers on an at-their-own-risk basis, to help identify any last remaining bugs, glitches and conflicts.

BINARY

Numbering system with a base of 2, where values are represented by zeros and ones.

BIOS

Basic Input Output System, a program stored in a microchip memory on the PC motherboard that checks and configures the hardware, memory and disk drives, before the operating system is loaded.

BITMAP

Type of image file format (extension *.bmp) used by Windows and many other programs; quality is high because no compression is used; however, bitmap files can be very large and are unsuitable for sending via e-mail.

BITRATE

A measure of the amount of digital data a system can process, measured in bits per second or 'bps', in the context of MP3 faster bit rates mean lower compression and higher sound quality.

BITS PER SECOND (bps)

The number of bits per second a serial communications system can handle determines how fast information can be conveyed from one point to another.

BOOLEAN

A branch of algebra named after nineteenth-century British mathematician George Boole.

BROWNOUT

A large reduction in the mains supply voltage, causing lights to dim and electronic devices like PCs to stop working.

BROWSER

An Internet access program, such as Microsoft Internet Explorer or Netscape Navigator/Communicator.

BURN

The process of recording a CD or CD-ROM.

CACHE

Part of a computer's memory set aside for storing frequently-used data from a disk drive, speeding up the transfer of information.

CAD/CAM
Computer aided design/manufacture – applications that require a high performance visual display.

CD-R/RW
Recordable CD-ROM systems; CD-R uses disks that can be written to just once whilst CD-RW (read-write) disks can be recorded on and erased many times.

CHAT
When in a NetMeeting call you can communicate by typing text into a message window, which appears almost instantly on the recipient's screen.

CHIP SOCKETS
Most of the microchips used in a PC are soldered directly to the circuit boards but some, including the main processor and some memory components are mounted in sockets, so they can be easily replaced or upgraded.

CLEANER WIPES
Fabric cloths moistened with specially formulated cleaning and anti-static fluid, available from most office supply companies.

CLIENT
A PC or program used to access files on another PC on a network.

CLIP ART
Copyright-free pictures, icons, cartoons and graphics supplied with word processor programs, or available separately on disk or from thousands of websites on the Internet.

CLIPBOARD
Windows utility used to temporarily copy chunks of text, data, graphics or pictures. Once on the clipboard the item can be pasted into another part of the document, or transferred to any other Windows application with a copy and paste facility.

CMOS
Complimentary metal oxide semiconductor – family of low power microchips used to store and process the BIOS program.

COBOL
Common Business Oriented Language – programming language used in data processing and business applications.

COMPRESSION
A technique used to reduce the size of a file, making it smaller, more manageable and faster to download.

CONSUMABLES
Component in a printer, such as the ink cartridge or ribbon, which need to be replaced when it runs out or exceeds its life expectancy.

CORE FONTS
The basic set of fonts or typefaces that are installed and used by Windows 95/98.

COUNTER
Web page component that logs the number of visitors to a site.

COVER SHEET
Fax page that is sent before the fax message, giving details of the sender, recipient, date and time.

CPU
Central Processor Unit – the main microprocessor chip in a PC.

CRT
Cathode Ray Tube – TV type video display, basically a big glass bottle with all of the air sucked out. The image is formed on a layer of phosphor coating the side of the glass faceplate, which glows when struck by a stream of fast moving electrons.

DAISY-CHAIN
USB devices have two sockets so they can be connected together, one to the other, like a chain.

DATA CARTRIDGE
A cassette, similar to audio or video tape. (Some tape backup systems use DAT and 8mm audio and video cassettes.)

DATA FIELD
In the context of an address book a single item of information, i.e. a forename or surname, house number and street name, postcode, etc.

DATA SOURCE
A file used to store a particular type of information, such as names and addresses.

DAT
Digital Audio Tape, high quality recording system using even smaller matchbox-sized tape cassettes spooled with 4mm wide magnetic tape.

DCC
Direct Cable Connection, a Windows utility for connecting two PCs together so they can exchange files.

DECOMPRESS
Files sent over the Internet are often 'compressed' to make them smaller and faster to send. However, in order to use the files they have to be decompressed or extracted on the host PC. Some compressed files come with their own automatic extraction utility, others – usually with the extension *.zip – depend on a separate program on the PC to 'unzip' the files.

DEFRAGGING
Over time the files on a PC's hard disk drive become disorganised – 'defragging' the drive restores order and speeds up reading and writing data.

DEGAUSS
Literally de-magnetise. A coil around the outside of the picture tube induces a collapsing magnetic field that eradicates any magnetic build up on metal components inside the tube.

DIAL UP CONNECTION
Utility in Windows responsible for connecting a PC, via a modem, to the Internet.

DIGITAL CAMCORDER
Camcorder that uses the 'DVC' (Digital Video Cassette) recording system. Pocket-sized models are capable of very high picture and sound quality.

DIMM
Dual in-line memory module, usually with 168 connecting pins.

DISPLAY CARD
A plug-in adaptor card or circuitry incorporated into the motherboard that converts digital information into an analogue video signal that is fed to the monitor.

DLL
Dynamic Link Library, a data file containing data or information needed by a program. DLLs may be shared by a number of applications, in which case they are stored in a central location, such as the System folder in Windows.

DMA
Direct Memory Access – a means of transferring data quickly between the hard disk and the PC's memory.

DOMAIN
A group of computers, sharing a common address or identity, connected together by a network. Thus a desktop PC connected to the Internet via an Internet Service Provider is part of that ISP's 'domain'.

DOMAIN NAMES (TOP LEVEL)
.ac.uk
UK academic organisation.

.com
world-wide 'commercial' entities, individuals or companies.

.co.uk
UK-based commercial entity, individual or company.

.edu
assigned to higher level educational establishments, colleges, universities, etc.

.gov/.gov.uk

reserved for US and UK government agencies and organisations respectively and similar bodies in other countries when preceded by the relevant country code.

.mod.uk

UK Ministry of Defence establishment websites.

.net

organisations which are part of the Internet infrastructure – i.e. Internet Service Providers, etc.

.nhs.uk

UK national health service website.

.org,/org.uk

originally reserved for non-profit making organisations (charities, political bodies, professional institutions, trades unions, etc.) but now issued to some commercial enterprises.

.sch.uk

UK schools domain.

DOS/MS-DOS

Disk Operating System, a program that runs independently of Windows responsible for controlling disk drives, organising data and memory resources.

DOS MODE

The PC is 'booted' without Windows with DOS as the primary operating system.

DOT PITCH

A measure of the size and spacing of the coloured light-emitting phosphor dots or stripes that coat the inside of the screen. The current norm is around 0.28mm, higher performance CRTs have dot pitches of between 0.23 and 0.25mm transferred from the hard disk to the RAM memory chips.

DRIVER

Drivers are small programs that tell Windows 95 how to communicate with a particular piece of hardware, like a mouse, joystick or printer.

DTP

Desktop publishing – makeup and layout programs used to design pages in printed documents, magazines, newspapers, books and Internet websites.

DUPLEX PRINTING

Printing on both sides of a sheet of paper. A few printers can do this automatically; however in most cases it is necessary for the user to manually re-load the paper or papers, facing the other way and in the right order.

DVD

Digital Versatile Disk – new high capacity optical disk system with a capacity of up to 5.2Gb per disk (at the moment). DVD drives can also read CD-ROMs. DVD recordable or 'RAM' drives are now available.

ECP/EPP

Extended Capabilities Port/Enhanced Parallel Port; printer port settings that allow faster data transfer rates.

EDO RAM

Extended data out, random access memory, high-speed RAM chips used on recent PCs with specialised memory controllers.

EIDE

Enhanced Integrated Drive Electronics, disk drive interface and control system used on most recent PCs.

EISA/ISA EXPANSION SLOT

Extended Industry Standard Architecture, type of connector on a PC motherboard, used for expansion or adapter cards.

E-MAIL ATTACHMENT

An attachment is a file – other than plain text – sent with or as an e-mail message.

EMBEDDED COMMANDS

Cells in a spreadsheet or table can contain hidden instructions to perform calculations or carry out specific actions when data is entered.

EMBEDDED FONTS

Typeface information included in a file that allows fonts and character sets to be displayed that may not be on the host PC.

EMERGENCY RECOVERY DISK

A floppy disk created by Windows containing files that will allow your PC to boot up in DOS mode, plus various tools and utilities to assist recovery following a crash.

ENCRYPTION

Encryption or scrambling renders files unreadable by any conventional means without the correct decryption software and a unique 'key' code, which is needed to unlock the data.

ENGINE

A self-contained program designed to do a specific task that operates within a larger application.

EXE

Files ending in .exe are 'executable' which basically means they contain a program that will start when the .exe file is opened.

EXPANSION CARDS

Most PCs contain a set of small circuit boards, plugged into the main motherboard for controlling the video output, processing sounds or communicating with the outside world (modems and network cards).

FAQ

Frequently asked questions, a simple guide to a particular topic or subject area.

FAT 32

File Allocation Table – the indexing system used by the PC to control where and how data is stored on the hard disk. The FAT 32 system makes more efficient use of the storage space available and allows drives larger than 2Gb to function as a single drive.

FIELD

An area on a document that acts as a container for text or data that needs to be entered or might change, without affecting the rest of the document.

FILE EXTENSIONS (WINDOWS & POPULAR APPLICATIONS)

.avi

Audio-Video Interleaved, Microsoft standard movie files.

.bak

Backup or archive file, usually created automatically by a program.

.bmp

Bitmap, standard Windows image or graphics file.

.cab

Cabinet, compressed data file used on Microsoft software installation disks.

.dll

Dynamic Link Library, contains information or data that may be shared by several programs.

.doc

Microsoft Word document.

.exe

Executable, a file containing a program or instructions to start a program.

.gif

Graphics Interchange Format, a graphics file, mainly used on Internet web pages.

.hlp

Help file.

.htm/html

HyperText Markup Language, Internet web page files.

.ico

Windows icon files.

.ini

Initialisation file containing information needed to start and configure Windows.

.jpg/.jpeg
Joint Photographic Experts Group, compressed image file.

.lwp
Lotus Word Pro document.

.mid
Musical Instrument Digital interface, music file.

.mov
QuickTime Movie file.

.mp3
Moving Picture Expert Group 3, CD quality sound file used for music on the Internet.

.mpg/mpeg
Moving Picture Experts Group, video movie file.

.old
Convention for renaming old or disused files that may be needed at some time in the future.

.pdf
Portable Document Format, interactive text file with web-like links.

.rtf
Rich Text Format, industry standard text file, can be read by most word processors.

.scr
Screensaver file.

.sys
System file, containing information needed to load and configure Windows.

.tif/.tiff
Tagged Image Format File, graphics file.

.tmp
Temporary file, generated by Windows and various applications, normally deleted when the program or Windows is closed.

.ttf
True Type Font, file containing typeface information.

.txt
File containing plain or unformatted text.

.uue
Text file format used to send program files containing binary information by e-mail.

.wav
Waveform, windows sound file.

.wpd
Word Perfect document file.

.xls
Microsoft Excel worksheet.

.zip
File containing compressed binary data, used for sending programs or information on the Internet.

FILE FRAGMENTS
Files or bits of files left behind on the hard disk when a program is deleted.

FIREWIRE
(aka IEEE 1394) High-speed serial data connection system used on some high end PCs and laptops used for demanding video and graphics applications.

FLAME
Offensive or abusive e-mails, usually sent in response to someone infringing basic newsgroup netiquette.

FLATBED
Desktop scanner with horizontal (flat) picture/document holder, usually covered by a hinged top.

FLIP & ROTATE
An option in most graphics programs and word processors to rotate a text or graphics object on the page.

FOLLOW-UPS

A response to a newsgroup message or posting, which will form part of a 'thread' for others to read and reply to.

FONT/TYPEFACE

Text style and size. Virtually all word processors have a 'wizzywig' display (actually WYSIWYG, or what you see is what you get. . .) so what appears on the screen is what ends up on the printed page.

FORMAT

Process of preparing a disk drive to store data by organising a file structure so that information can be systematically written and retrieved by the PC's operating system.

FORMATTING

Process that prepares a disk for use by effectively deleting all of the data on it by creating a new filing structure.

FORMULA

Mathematical expressions, such as add, subtract, multiply and divide, used to create an instruction that tells a cell how to behave or process a piece of information.

FREEWARE

Shareware programs that are free to use, but the author retains control and copyright over the original programming code.

FTP

File Transfer Protocol, Internet system used to move data files from one computer to another.

FUNCTION KEYS

The row of keys along the top of the keyboard, which can be assigned to various functions in an open application (F1 traditionally calls up Help).

GAMEPORT

A 15-pin female connector socket designed exclusively for joysticks and other control devices.

GEOMETRY
The size and shape of the display on a monitor screen. Most monitors have controls to alter the vertical and horizontal position and the linearity of the top and sides (sometimes called trapezoid adjustment). Some models also have a tilt control, to ensure the display aligns with the edges of the screen, to compensate for the Earth's magnetic field and local influences.

GIF
Graphics Interchange Format – standard file format for images and graphics used on Internet web pages.

GPF
General Protection Fault – a 'fatal' software error, causing a running program to stop working because it fights (and loses) over the amount of memory resources it and other programs have been allocated by Windows.

GRAPHIC EQUALISER
Sophisticated tone control, for precisely setting bass, mid-range and treble frequencies during playback on an audio system.

gsm
Grams per square metre, measurement of paper weight and consequently thickness. Standard copier paper is usually 80 to 100 gsm, thin card starts at around 120gsm.

GSM
Global System for Mobile communications – digital cellular telephone system used by the Cellnet and Vodaphone networks in the UK and in more than 100 other countries.

GUTTER
The blank space between the inner margins of two facing pages in a magazine, newspaper or book.

HEXADECIMAL
Numbering system used by computers, with a base of 16, represented by the numbers 0 to 9 and the letters A to F.

HIBERNATION MODE

The PC is 'asleep', with the disk drives dormant and Windows and running programs suspended, but the processor is still active and the system can be revived in just a few seconds by pre-determined actions (mouse or keyboard activity, modem ring, etc.).

HIGH SPEED GRAPHICS

Multimedia computers are great for fast action games but they can actually be too quick for applications like word processors. When scrolling through a document the display can move so fast that it's almost impossible to read the text.

HITS

Search results, usually a brief summary of a website's contents, the site address, a relevance rating and an underlined link to click on, to take you to the site.

HOST

An Internet company providing storage space for websites on their server computer.

HOST COMPUTER

A computer – usually part of a wider network, like the Internet – that is accessed by one or more users at remote terminals.

HOT KEYS

A combination of two or three keystrokes that activates a command or a program.

HOT PLUG/SWAP

Connecting a device or peripheral to a PC whilst one or both are switched on.

HTML

Hypertext Mark-up Language – hidden codes in text documents, web pages and e-mails that allow the reader to quickly move about the document, or jump to another, by clicking on underlined 'links' which appear as coloured highlighted words or phrases.

HTTP

HyperText Transfer Protocol – a set of rules that governs how text is displayed on Internet documents plus a means of moving around inside documents and accessing other web pages by clicking on highlighted or underlined links.

HUB

A multi-way connector with one input and several outputs.

HYPERLINK

Highlighted and underlined text or icon on a web page, clicking on the 'link' takes you to another part of the document, or another web page.

ILS

Internet Locator Server – an Internet site or server that allows users logged on to that site to communicate with one another, either individually or in groups.

INBOX

A folder created by Outlook Express where all of your incoming mail messages are stored.

INCREMENTAL BACKUP

A backup strategy that only records the changes made to chosen files.

INTERNAL STORAGE

Many non-PC e-mail devices cannot store e-mail messages as they have limited memory capacity: instead messages are kept on the server computer, though there may be a limit to the number of messages, and the space that they occupy and in some cases old messages will be deleted to make way for new ones.

IP ADDRESS

Internet Protocol Address – unique 32-bit code, represented by four groups of digits, used to identify websites and Internet users.

IR

Infrared, cordless serial data communications systems used on many laptops and peripherals and a number of cellphones. The common standard is known as IrDA (Infrared Data Association).

IrDA
Infrared Data Association, the organisation responsible for setting and maintaining technical standards for IR wireless communications systems used on PCs and peripherals.

IRQ
Interrupt Request – a set of instructions that enable the processor to manage a succession of tasks in sequence.

ISA
Industry Standard Architecture – connection system used on IBM PCs and compatibles, for plug-in 'daughter boards' such as sound and video cards and modems, etc.

ISP
Internet Service Provider – a company providing Internet access, an e-mail address and a mailbox where messages sent to you are stored before they're downloaded on to your PC.

JAVA
A versatile Internet programming language used in a wide range of applications, including creating animation and web page forms.

JPEG
Joint Photographic Experts Group – part of International Standards Organisations, responsible for devising software compression systems. Picture file format used for storing photographs, data is compressed thus saving space and reducing download times on Internet pages and e-mails.

KEYBOARD SHORTCUT
A simple and ideally memorable sequence of two or three keystrokes, used to invoke a frequently used action or activity within a program or application.

KEY CAPS
Press-fit embossed keys tops on a PC keyboard.

KEYWORDS
Words or phrases that elicit a programmed response from a software application.

LAN
Local Area Network – a computer network where all of the PCs are physically close to one another in the same room, office or building.

LASERDISC
Now virtually obsolete, the limited storage capacity of the LP-sized disks meant films had to be recorded on both sides of the disk or on two disks.

LCD
Liquid crystal display – flat panel display used on laptop and portable PC and now available for desktop machines. LCD monitors consume far less power than CRTs and generate no harmful emissions. The image is made up of tens of thousands of picture elements or 'pixels' that can be switched on and off to control the passage of light.

LOG FILE
A record of the name and location of all the files stored on the hard disk, and any alterations made to other files, during software installation.

MACHINE CODE
The basic language of computers, usually a form of binary code, where instructions are represented by groups of 'ones' and 'zeros'.

MACRO
Simple programming function in Word (and many other programs) used to automate frequently used commands and functions.

MAILBOX
Storage space on an ISP's server computer where incoming e-mail messages are stored prior to them being downloaded and read on your PC.

MAIL MERGE
Word facility to help automate the process of printing form letters, envelopes and address labels.

MESSAGE RULES
A facility in Outlook Express that automatically ignores or disposes of e-mail messages from nominated addresses/senders.

MIME
Multipurpose Internet Mail Extensions, a widely used system for converting non-text files and information – images, HTML commands, etc. – to and from plain text so it can be sent as e-mail.

MIRROR SITE
A website containing a duplicate set of archives or data – usually geographically distant to the parent site – to help relieve strain on busy sites and net infrastructure.

MODEM
MOdulator/DEModulator, a device that converts digital signals coming from your PC into audible tones that can be sent via a conventional telephone line.

MOTHERBOARD
The main printed circuit board inside a PC, containing the main processor chip (Pentium, etc.) memory chips (RAM) and plug-in expansion cards or 'daughter' boards.

MOVIE CLIPS
Short low-resolution video sequences can be 'attached' to an e-mail message; however, the image is generally small, jerky and of relatively poor quality.

MP3
Motion Picture Experts Group audio layer 3 – digital audio compression system commonly used to send files containing audio and music over the Internet.

MPEG-2
Moving Pictures Expert Group – MPEG-2 is one of a set of technical standards for compressing video into digital data; picture quality is at least as good as normal broadcast TV.

MS-DOS

Microsoft Disk Operating System, a program, using text-based commands that works beside Windows to control the way disk drives handle and process information.

NAG SCREEN

A window or display that appears when a program has started to remind the user to pay a registration fee or indicate how many days of the trial period remain.

NEWSGROUP

Public notice boards on the Internet where like-minded net users can post e-mail messages, articles or announcements for others to read and respond to.

NICAM

Near Instantaneously Companded Audio Multiplexing, since you ask... The digital stereo TV sound system used by UK TV broadcasters.

NODE

A 'location' in a network, either a computer or a peripheral device, with its own unique address.

NON-VOLATILE MEMORY

A memory chip that retains data when the power supply is removed.

NULL MODEM

Type of serial communications cable, configured for two-way data transfer between a PC and a modem, or two PCs.

NUMBER FORMAT

A set of styles, that decide how numbers, symbols and mathematical expressions are presented.

OCR

Optical Character Recognition – software that converts an image into a text file by identifying patterns of alphanumeric characters.

OFFICE ASSISTANT

Help feature in Word where a 'friendly' cartoon character pops up and tells you how to do things. For example typing 'Dear Sir' will bring up advice on how to write a letter.

ON-SCREEN KEYBOARD

A virtual keyboard where characters are selected using a mouse pointer or other means, such as voice control or movement.

OPERATING SYSTEM

A collection of programs, such as Windows 95, 98 and DOS (disk operating system) which manage all of your PC's resources – RAM memory, disk drive, display screen, etc. – and controls how files are stored and retrieved.

OSR2

Original equipment manufacturer Service Release 2, the later version of Windows 95 supplied to PC manufacturers, incorporating many of the features of Windows 98 (including FAT 32). This was not sold separately by Microsoft but it is widely available from 'friendly' dealers and through ads in computer magazines.

OVERTYPE

Typing a letter or character replaces the character or space next to it.

PACKET

Data travelling around the Internet is chopped up by the server computers and sent in brief bursts or packets, to be reassembled by the software on the end-user's PC.

PAPER PATH

The rollers and guides inside a printer through which sheets of paper pass.

PAPER WEIGHT

Paper weight and thickness of paper is measured in grams per square metre (gsm). Ordinary copier/printing paper is normally between 80 and 85gsm; lightweight card is in the range 200 to 300gsm.

PARALLEL PORT

One of the rear panel connections on your PC (or laptop) usually used by printers and scanners. Data is transferred relatively quickly 4 or 8 bits at a time.

PARTITION

Dividing a large disk drive up into partitions or virtual drives gets around capacity limitations imposed by an operating system or the drive's own control system.

PATCH

A program or file intended to fix or work around a problem in a software application.

PATH

The location of a file or program on a hard disk, e.g. to specify the file that starts Microsoft Word the path might be: C:\Program Files\Microsoft Office\Office\Winword.exe.

PC-CARD ADAPTOR

Credit card sized modules (but a little thicker) used in laptops for modems, memory expansion and other peripherals. Adaptor modules have slots for memory cards.

PCI

Peripheral Component Interconnect – high-speed connector and control system, used on most recent PCs, also used for sound, video, adaptor cards.

PCMCIA

Personal Computer Memory Card International Association. Body responsible for PC card standards. PC cards are credit card sized modules (but a little thicker) used in laptops for modems, memory expansion and other peripherals.

PCN

Personal Communications Network (aka GSM 1800) digital cellular telephone system used by Orange, One 2 One and Virgin in the UK and more than 100 other countries.

PERSONAL PASSWORD

The password chosen by you, or issued to you when you opened your Internet and e-mail account.

PHOTO VIEWER

Program that allows you to view the contents of folders containing image files, usually as small 'thumbnails', which can then be displayed full size.

PIXEL

Picture-Element, a single dot in a digitally generated image or display, the greater the number of pixels the greater the amount of detail.

PLATEN

The glass plate on a flatbed scanner onto which documents are placed.

POP3

Post Office Protocol version 3 – widely used Internet e-mail standard, compatible with popular Windows 'client' software (Outlook, Outlook Express, MS Exchange/Windows Messaging, Eudora, etc.) on PCs and palmtop computers (Psion, Windows CE, etc.).

POWER MANAGEMENT

Windows utilities that help to reduce power consumption by switching off components when they are not being used. It can be disabled by clicking on the Power Management icon in Control Panel (Start > Settings, or Control Panel icon in My Computer).

POWER SUPPLY MODULE

The power supply module converts mains electricity into a low voltage DC, needed by the motherboard and disk drives. It's normally housed inside a metal box, fitted with a cooling fan, attached to the back of the case or system unit.

PROFILE

Windows facility (see Passwords in Control Panel) that allows several users to share a PC, setting up their own custom preferences and desktop settings.

QIC

Quarter Inch Committee; standards organisation responsible for devising data.

RAM

Random Access Memory, a computer's working memory, where programs store data and information when they are running.

REFRESH RATE

Like a TV picture, the display on a PC monitor is 'redrawn' may times each second but our eyes and brain perceive it as a single continuous image. If the image is redrawn less than 75 times a second some people may perceive a slight flicker.

REGISTRY

A large, constantly changing file in Windows 95/98 and ME containing details of how your PC is set up and configuration information for all the programs stored on the hard disk.

REN

Ringer Equivalence Number – all devices (modems, fax machines, answering machines, etc.) that can be connected to the public switched telephone network (PTSN) are required to have a REN number. This determines how many other devices can be connected to the same line. Most phone lines can support a REN of 4. If it is any higher some devices may not function correctly.

RESOLUTION

A measure of how much fine detail a video screen can display. To change the setting on a Windows PC go to Start > Settings > Control Panel, select the Display icon and the Settings tab.

RESPONSE BOX

A blank area or box on a form for text or data entry.

RIBBON CABLE

Flat multi-way cable, used inside a PC to connect disk drives to the main motherboard or plug-in controller cards.

ROM/PROM/EPROM

Read Only Memory/Programmable Read Only Memory/Erasable Programmable Read Only Memory; a 'non-volatile' memory chip that retains information when the power is removed. Information in ROMs and PROMs is fixed whilst an EPROM can be re-programmed with new data.

RTFM

Read The Flipping Manual (or something very similar. . .).

RULES

A set of conditions, decided on by the user that decide how e-mail messages are processed. E-mails from a particular person or address might be routed to a separate folder or 'flagged' with an on-screen indicator. Junk e-mail from a nominated address or containing a specified keyword can be sent straight to the waste bin.

SAFE MODE

Special Windows diagnostic mode used to help trace faults by loading a minimum configuration, avoiding sometimes-troublesome start-up files and drivers.

SCANDISK

Windows utility that checks the integrity of data stored on a hard disk drive, identifies problems, and where possible, puts them right.

SCANNER

Device attached to a computer that converts a photograph or image into digital data, stored on the PC as an image file.

SCREEN GRAB

A snapshot of the PC's video display, copied to the Windows Clipboard as a bitmap file. Pressing PrintScreen captures the whole screen, Alt + PrintScreen grabs just the active window.

SDRAM

Synchronous dynamic random access memory, another family of memory chips that allows data to be accessed at higher speeds.

SEARCH ENGINE
Internet sites that seek out information, by topic, keyword or name. Good places to start a name search are: www.google.com, www.yahoo.com www.lycos.com and www.altavista.com.

SEARCH FIELD
The space in a search engine where you type in keywords, a short phrase or question.

SELF-EXTRACTING
A compressed program or file that contains its own 'unzip' utility.

SERIAL PORT
Most PCs have two serial ports. One may be used by the mouse, the other by an external modem. Data is transferred relatively slowly, one bit at a time.

SERVER
Fast, powerful computers with vast storage capacity, used to communicate and share data with other computers connected to local or large-scale networks.

SHAREWARE
Software programs that you can try, before you buy. If you decide to use it you are obliged to send a payment to the author or publisher. Some programs are automatically disabled when the trial period has expired.

SIMM
Single in-line memory module, with 30 or 72 connecting pins.

SIZING HANDLES
Highlights – usually small black squares around the edge of a graphic object or picture – that can be used to change its size and shape by clicking and dragging the mouse pointer.

SMTP
Simple Mail Transfer Protocol – system used to move e-mail messages around the Internet.

SNAPSHOT
A compilation of data and statistics about your PC including details of the operating system, memory resources and status and running programs.

SOHO
Small Office, Home Office, a category of PC peripherals and office equipment designed for light to medium workloads.

SOUNDCARD
A more or less standard fitment on modern desktop PCs, generating the sounds and music heard through the PC's speakers. Most sound cards also have a microphone input, necessary for voice recognition.

SPIKES, SURGES & TRANSIENTS
Brief increases in mains voltage, varying from a few volts to several thousand volts.

SPLASH SCREEN
An image or logo that appears on a PC screen whilst a program is loading.

SPOOL
Simultaneous Peripheral Operations On-Line; a way of maximising PC and printer efficiency. Information to be printed is transferred to a temporary file, so the PC can get on with other jobs, and carry on printing when it has a moment to spare.

SSL
Secure Sockets Layer, a powerful encryption system used to send data and information, like credit card details, over the Internet.

STANDBY
PCs with motherboards that support the Standby function, switch to a low power mode when the standby function is engaged. A variety of actions, including mouse clicks, key presses, or signals from the modem wakes up the PC.

START-UP FOLDER
Folder containing programs that load automatically after Windows.

STREAMING

Technique used to send sound and pictures over the Internet. Data is 'buffered' or stored in a temporary memory by player software on the PC to minimise the interruptions that would otherwise occur as data on the net is sent in chunks or 'packets'.

SURGES AND SPIKES

Potentially damaging high voltage transients carried on the mains supply and on telephone lines.

SWITCH

An extra instruction (or instructions) added to the end of a DOS command.

SYSTEM FILES

Important files that configure Windows during boot up, telling the operating system what settings to use, what software is loaded and the hardware or peripherals attached to the PC.

SYSTEM TRAY

Area on the far right of the Windows Taskbar reserved for running applications, frequently used utilities and the desktop clock.

TEMP FILES

Temporary files, ending in '.tmp' are created by Windows and other programs and normally deleted automatically though some will remain if Windows crashes or is not shut down properly.

TEMPLATE

A ready prepared document or layout that can be easily modified or personalised by changing sample text and graphics.

THREAD

Messages in a newsgroup, forum or on a bulletin board linked by a common theme.

THUMBNAIL PREVIEW

Reduced-sized image, quicker to load and display and cuts down on memory resources.

TIME-LIMITED
Programs with a built-in time switch, which will stop it functioning after a pre-set period – usually 30 days – after it was installed.

TLD
Top Level Domain – the part of a website address, after the second or third 'dot' that denotes the site owner's status (i.e. .com for commercial entity, .org for non-profit making organisations like charities, etc.) or country where the site is based (.uk for UK, .fr for France, etc.).

TOOLS
Small programs or applications that modify or change the way things work or happen on a PCDOMAIN, the unique name that identifies an Internet site.

TRACKBALL
A kind of upside-down mouse, where screen pointer movement is controlled by moving a large ball.

TRANSCEIVER
Combined transmitter-receiver.

TRIAL/DEMO PROGRAMS
Programs distributed by software manufacturers that allow potential users to try before they buy. Some key functions may be disabled or the program is 'time-limited' and will stop working after the trial period. Trial programs can usually be unlocked with a 'key' issued by the manufacturer, who will also provide support and updates, when the program has been purchased.

TROJAN
Potentially destructive program, often masquerading as a normal application that can also allow unauthorised external access to files and data on PCs connected to networks and the Internet.

TWEAK UI
Unsupported Microsoft utility program for making detailed changes to the way Windows looks and behaves by editing the Registry.

UNINSTALLER
A program removal utility included with a lot of Windows software; programs with uninstallers are usually (but not always) listed in Add/Remove Programs in Control Panel.

UNLOCK CODE
Shareware that is time-limited or has restricted functionality can be fully enabled with an unlock code, sent to the user by e-mail from the author or publisher once they have received the appropriate fee – usually by on-line credit card payment.

URL
Uniform Resource Locator – a standard Internet address, e.g. http://www.telegraph.co.uk.

USB
Universal Serial Bus, high-speed industry standard connection system for peripherals including monitors, modems, joysticks, printers, etc., that does away with confusing technicalities and allows 'hot swaps', allowing connection and disconnection with the PC switched on.

USENET
A network of server computers used to distribute the 'official' Newsgroups on the Internet.

VA
Volt-Ampere, a measure of electricity supply and generation. You can work out the required capacity of a UPS by adding up the power consumption figures (RMS values measured in watts) of your PC monitor, etc., into a VA figure by multiplying it by 1.414.

VGA
Video Graphics Array – standard display format used on PCs, typically made up of 640 × 400 pixels and 256 colours.

VIDEO CAPTURE CARD
PC expansion card that converts analogue video – from a camcorder, TV tuner, VCR, etc. – into digital data, that can be processed on a PC. Some

cards also convert PC video back to analogue, for recording on a VCR or display on a TV. Digital video capture cards are also available for digital camcorders with FireWire digital video connections.

VIRUS
Unauthorised program or executable code that can be hidden inside legitimate programs and e-mail messages, often capable of self-replication, that can cause a range of effects, from prank messages to corruption and deletion of files and complete system failure.

VISUALBASIC & WORDBASIC
Text-based programming languages used to create macros.

VOICE SYNTHESISER
Software that converts text – including menu options and commands – appearing on the PC screen into speech.

WAP
Wireless Application Protocol – new generation of Internet compatible digital mobile phones capable of sending and receiving e-mail messages.

WAV
Short for waveform; the file extension .wav denotes digital sound files used by Windows and most Windows games and applications.

WEB CAM
A small video camera that plugs into your PC (most budget models use the universal serial bus – USB – port).

WEB HOST
Company providing disk space on its server computer for a website. Most Internet Service Providers allocate a small amount of free web space for their subscribers (typically 10 to 20Mb); larger amounts of space generally have to be paid for.

WEB MAIL
E-mail messages can be sent to and from web sites, bypassing the need for special software. The best-known service is Hotmail, which offers free e-mail accounts at www.hotmail.com.

WET CLEANERS
Disk drive cleaners that use a liquid agent (usually isopropyl alcohol) to remove dirt and dust from the read/write heads or laser pickups.

WHITEBOARD
Facility in NetMeeting that opens a blank page that you can write or sketch on and is immediately seen on your contact's screen.

WILDCARD
A wildcard is an asterisk '*' which in PC language means literally anything. In this context a wildcard in place of the first part of an Internet address – e.g. *.com – signifies all addresses ending in .com.

WINDOWS NT
Windows New Technology, highly stable but less well featured version of the Windows operating system, designed for critical business and network applications.

WIZARD
Simple help program that automatically starts when you begin a task.

WORDBASIC
Simple text-based programming language used by Word, to control various behind-the-scenes functions and features. (BASIC = beginners all-purpose symbolic instruction code.)

WORM
A type of virus, usually hidden inside another program, designed to penetrate a computer's operating system. Once activated it is programmed to replicate and attach itself to other programs or e-mails.

WRITING SPEED
Current norms are 300 and 600 kilobits/second or ×2 and ×4 'normal' speed. Faster (and dearer) drives can achieve speeds of ×8 and ×12.

ZIP
Type of compressed file, requires special program (Pkunzip, WinZip, etc.) to expand or decompress the file.

Index